WILD WORLD

A CLOSE UP LOOK AT LIFE IN THE EARTH'S WILDEST PLACES

JINNY JOHNSON

BARNES
& NOBLE
BOOKS
NEW YORK

Contents

A harpy eagle swoops
upon a group of
surprised monkeys

Introduction

Hot, wet forests, alive with monkeys and parrots, vast sandy deserts, icy lands and huge oceans—these are some of the wonders of the natural world. Our world can be divided into a number of natural areas. Each one is different, according to how hot or cold it is, how much rain falls and the types of plants and animals that live there.

Hotter and wetter than anywhere else on earth are the tropical rainforests. Lots of plants grow in these forests and provide food and shelter for an amazing variety of animals from flying frogs to gorillas. Deserts are some of the driest parts of the world, but a surprising number of animals, such as gerbils and even a snake, burrow in the sand to escape the heat of the day.

The poles are the coldest places on Earth. Some animals such as polar bears hunt on land and many kinds of birds and seals find food in the icy waters. Oceans, covering two thirds of the Earth, are the largest of the natural areas, home to thousands of kinds of fish and other animals.

Each chapter of this book explores one of these natural areas. A map shows where in the world it is found and the following pages look at some of the fascinating animals that live there and the incredible ways that they have adapted to their surroundings.

Desert scorpion

Blue morpho butterfly

Flower mantis

Minke whale

Orca whale

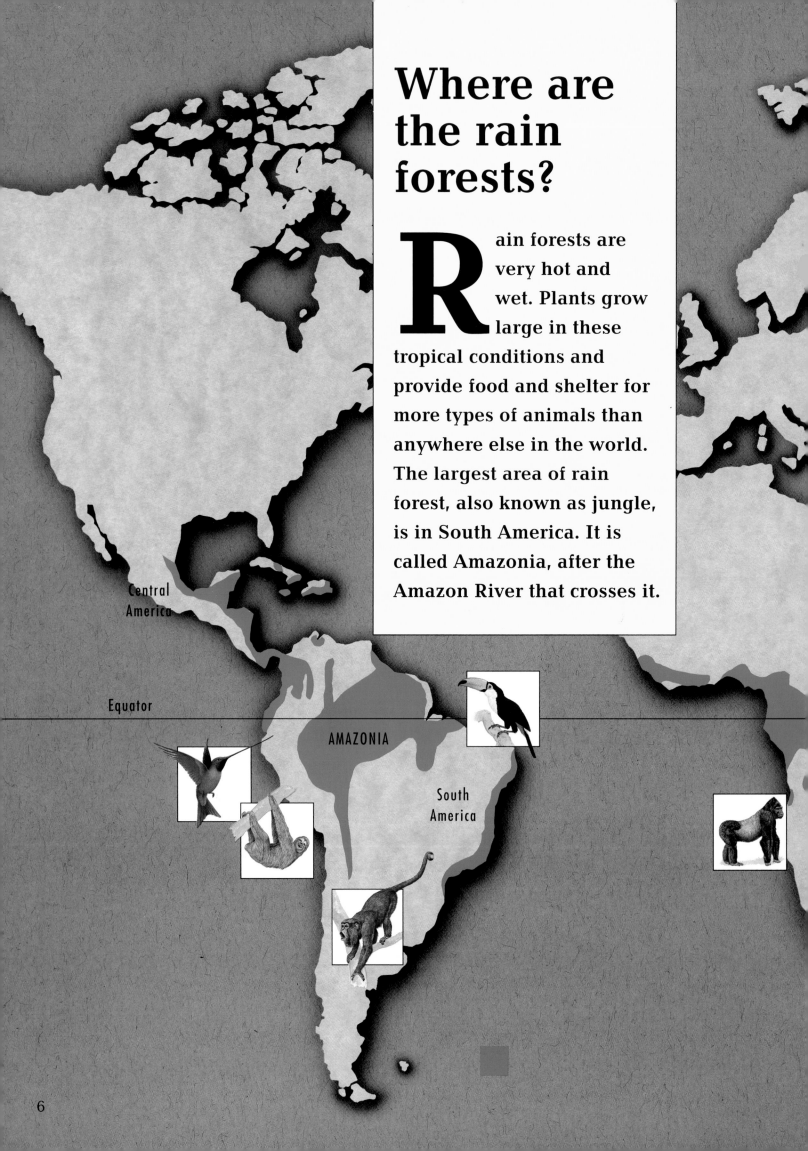

Where are the rain forests?

Rain forests are very hot and wet. Plants grow large in these tropical conditions and provide food and shelter for more types of animals than anywhere else in the world. The largest area of rain forest, also known as jungle, is in South America. It is called Amazonia, after the Amazon River that crosses it.

Central America

Equator

AMAZONIA

South America

India

Sri Lanka

Africa

Southeast
Asia

New Guinea

Madagascar

Australia

Living in the rain forest

Countless creatures, including frogs, birds, monkeys, snakes, and insects, live in the rain forest. On just one tree there may be 900 different types of beetles! Each layer of the forest has its own particular animal life.

Layers of the jungle

These are the layers into which the rain forest is divided. The animals illustrated here represent the wide variety of creatures that live in the different rain forests of the world.

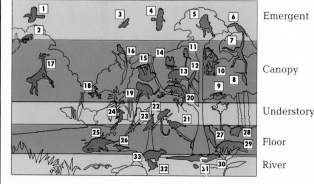

Emergent

Canopy

Understory

Floor

River

1 Great hornbill	12 Blue bird of paradise	23 Emerald tree boa
2 Pygmy glider	13 Tree porcupine	24 Aye-aye
3 Birdwing butterfly	14 Eclectus parrots	25 Giant armadillo
4 Harpy eagle	15 Three-toed sloth	26 Satin bowerbird
5 Proboscis monkey	16 Quetzal	27 Gorilla
6 Toco toucan	17 Black spider monkey	28 Jaguar
7 Gibbon	18 Wallace's flying frog	29 Giant anteater
8 Hummingbird	19 Red howler monkey	30 Spectacled caiman
9 Flying lemur	20 Tree anteater	31 Red piranha
10 Paradise tree snake	21 Great curassow	32 Fisherman bat
11 Golden lion tamarin	22 Tree kangaroo	33 Capybara

The jungle river teems with fish, including the flesh-eating piranha. Many other creatures, such as the guinea-piglike capybara and the caiman, live in or near the river.

Reaching high above the rest of the forest are some very tall trees. The tops of these form what is called the **emergent** layer, home to some birds and butterflies—and the proboscis monkey.

A mass of green treetops makes an almost unbroken layer of leaves and branches. This is the canopy layer and the busiest part of the forest, where many monkeys, birds, and insects live.

Below the main canopy, smaller trees, bushes, and tangled vines make up the understory layer. Here live small animals, such as aye-ayes and tree kangaroos, that have hands and feet designed for gripping branches.

On the dark forest floor, large animals, such as the giant anteater, root around for plants and insects to eat. Others, such as the gorilla, clamber into the trees to find food.

The tallest trees

At the very top of the jungle, in the trees that stand high above the rest of the forest, live eagles—some of the fiercest hunters. These powerful birds, such as the harpy and the monkey-eating eagles, hover above the canopy waiting to make lightning-quick dashes after monkeys or other prey.

The big-beaked toucans and hornbills also live up high, and many insects, including giant birdwing butterflies, dart among the branches. The rare proboscis monkey is one of the few large animals to live at this height.

With the help of its sharp hooked beak and strong claws, the **Philippine monkey-eating eagle** hunts flying lemurs as well as monkeys.

The **great hornbill** has a long beak that it uses to reach food, such as fruits and insects. Despite its size, the beak is surprisingly light.

High-flying **morpho butterflies** have shimmering, brilliantly colored wings. These flash in the sunlight as the butterflies flit among the highest branches of the forest trees.

Pygmy gliders feed on insects, nectar, and pollen. They can glide from branch to branch with the help of flaps of skin at the sides of their bodies.

The **toucan's** rainbow-bright beak may look clumsy, but it helps the bird find food in the Amazon rain forest. The toucan can reach small berries and other fruits at the ends of branches with the tip of its 8-inch-long beak.

When the **proboscis monkey** makes its loud honking call, its long, fleshy nose straightens out. This may even make the sound louder.

The harpy eagle can chase prey through the trees at a speed of 50 miles an hour.

The largest and most powerful eagle in the world, the harpy is about 3 feet long and has clawed feet the size of a man's hand. It feeds mainly on monkeys and sloths. Once the harpy has caught its victim, it removes all the animal's fur before eating it.

GUESS WHAT?...

Birdwings are among the biggest butterflies in the world. Some are up to 8 inches wide—almost as wide as this page. Although they live in the tallest trees, birdwings do come down to lower layers to feed on flower nectar.

The sloth spends so much of its life hanging upside down that its hair grows the opposite way to that of most animals.

Sloths have long, thin hands and feet with strong, curving claws. These claws act like hooks, and the sloth uses them to hang from branches. There are two kinds of sloths—the two-toed and the three-toed.

In the treetops

The almost unbroken mass of treetops of the jungle canopy makes another world high above the ground. This is home to many birds as well as lots of good climbers, including monkeys and gibbons. Like the tree anteater, many of these climbers have a special grasping tail. This prehensile tail, as it is called, acts like an extra leg that the animal can use to hold onto branches.

The **king vulture** feeds mostly on dead animals. It has a much keener sense of smell than most birds, which helps it find food in the dense rain forest.

Like all gibbons, the acrobatic **black gibbon** uses its long arms and hands to swing through the trees at great speed. The arms of the black gibbon are twice the length of its body and touch the ground when it stands upright on its back legs.

Praying mantises often look very much like leaves. This helps hide them from enemies—and prey. This leaflike praying mantis stays very still as it lies in wait for a passing insect.

By beating its wings very fast, the **sword-billed hummingbird** can hover in midair in front of flowers while it feeds on the sweet nectar inside. When hummingbirds hover, they use up lots of energy. If you worked this hard, you would have to eat as many as 130 loaves of bread a day to get enough energy.

A big, strong ape, the **orangutan** can walk along branches with ease or swing from branch to branch with its long arms. Fruit is its main food, but it also eats birds and their eggs.

The **tree anteater** has a long, sticky tongue that it uses to trap insects such as ants and termites.

Diana monkeys live in troops, or bands, of about thirty and spend nearly all their lives high in the trees. They eat leaves, fruits, and insects.

13

Many brilliantly colored birds dart among the branches of the rain forest canopy. There are plenty of seeds, fruits, and flowers in the canopy for plant-eating birds—and prey for birds that hunt for their food. Noisy parrots clamber among the branches, often using their beaks to help them hold on. And their short, broad wings allow them to fly among the closely packed trees.

Parrots are not the only noisy animals in the canopy. The call of the howler monkey of the Amazon jungle is one of the loudest of any land animal.

A strong, gripping tail helps the **tree porcupine** hold onto branches as it climbs. Its spiny body helps protect it from enemies.

Red howler monkeys have amazingly loud voices. They live in groups of about eight, and the leading male monkey shouts at other howlers to keep them away from his group's territory.

Few male and female birds look so different from one another as **eclectus parrots**. The female has mostly red feathers, while the male is green with blue and red patches.

14

Silky golden fur covers the little **golden lion tamarin**. This acrobatic creature bounds from branch to branch, searching for small birds, insects, and fruits to eat.

Male **quetzals** have colorful tail feathers that are up to twice the length of their body. These splendid feathers help the quetzal attract a mate.

The male blue bird of paradise shows off to his female mate by hanging upside down from a branch.

All birds of paradise live in the jungles of New Guinea. They fly high in the jungle canopy and eat fruits, insects, and spiders. The males have brilliantly colored feathers.

GUESS WHAT?...

Macaws, such as the **scarlet macaw,** have extra-strong hooked beaks for cracking open nuts to eat. They also eat leaves and fruits. Like all parrots, scarlet macaws make screeching calls as they fly, often in family groups or flocks of up to twenty.

Tree-living animals sometimes want to move around the forest. But it is a long way from the canopy down to the forest floor. Instead of climbing up and down the tall tree trunks, some animals can glide from one tree to another, using their bodies like parachutes. Animals such as frogs and lizards are able to "fly" in this way.

Other creatures spend their whole lives in "mini-worlds" such as those provided by bromeliads and other large-leafed plants. Here they can find water, food, and shelter.

Even a snake can "fly." The **paradise tree snake** can flatten its body and glide through the air, steering itself with "swimming" movements.

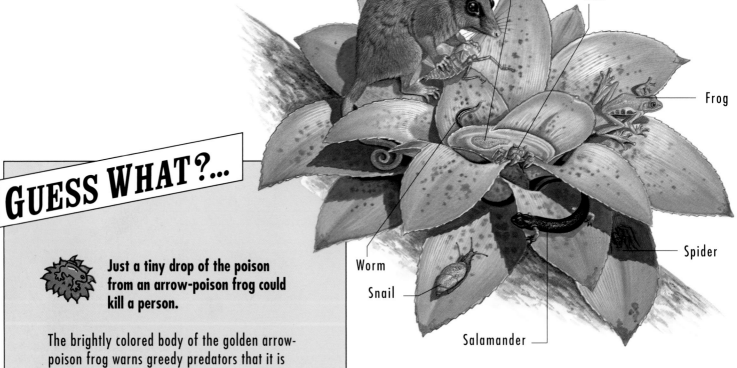

Mouse opossum

Dragonfly larva

Crab

Frog

Spider

Salamander

Snail

Worm

Bromeliads are plants with wide, thick leaves that live on the branches of trees in the rain forest. Rain water collects in the cuplike center—a very large plant can contain as much as 12 gallons of water. Tiny crabs, insects, and worms spend much of their lives in and around this mini-world. Salamanders, frogs, and insects come to the plant to lay their eggs in the water. And mouse opossums know that the bromeliad is a good place to catch insects.

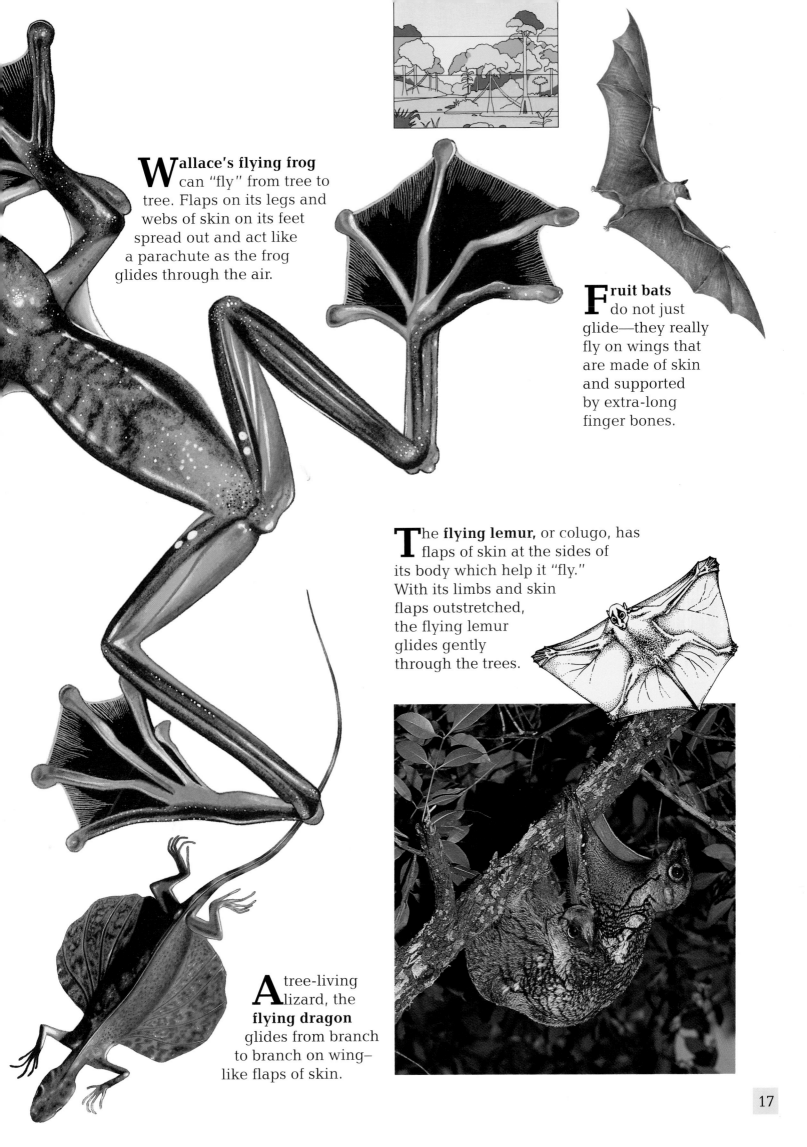

Wallace's flying frog can "fly" from tree to tree. Flaps on its legs and webs of skin on its feet spread out and act like a parachute as the frog glides through the air.

Fruit bats do not just glide—they really fly on wings that are made of skin and supported by extra-long finger bones.

The **flying lemur,** or colugo, has flaps of skin at the sides of its body which help it "fly." With its limbs and skin flaps outstretched, the flying lemur glides gently through the trees.

A tree-living lizard, the **flying dragon** glides from branch to branch on wing–like flaps of skin.

Deep in the forest

The little **potto** sleeps in the trees by day and hunts at night. Although it moves slowly, the potto still manages to grab fast-moving insects in its strong hands.

Below the main jungle canopy of tall trees there is a layer of smaller trees and bushes called the understory. Here many vines and other climbing plants twine around the trees and make a very thick mass of leaves and branches.

Most of the animals that live in the understory are small and light, like the lorises and pottos, and have hands and feet suited to holding onto branches.

Although it is a large bird, the **curassow** moves quickly through the trees. Its big, strong feet help it run along branches.

Chimpanzees are good climbers and find much of their food, such as fruits, nuts, and leaves, in the trees. At night they usually sleep in the trees in nests made from broken and bent branches.

There is even a
tree-living kangaroo in the jungle.

The tree kangaroo lives in the Australian rain forest. It eats fruits and leaves and, like other kangaroos, has a pouch for its young.

GUESS WHAT?...

White rings around its eyes give this jungle owl its name of **spectacled owl.** But young birds have brown spectacle markings and mostly white feathers. This owl eats birds, lizards, and other small animals.

Blotchy markings help keep the **golden cat** hidden among the leaves and branches as it searches for prey. It is about twice the size of a domestic cat.

The **slender loris** has special muscles that allow it to grip onto branches for hours without getting tired. It can even hang by just one leg as it feeds.

The **aye-aye** has an extra-long finger on each hand. This finger is used to pull insects from tree bark. The aye-aye's hearing is so good that it can hear insects below the bark.

The lower levels of the rain forest are dark and gloomy because the taller trees above block out so much light. But plenty of plants do manage to grow there. Some have such beautiful, glossy leaves that they have become popular indoor plants.

Thousands of different types of snakes, lizards, frogs, and insects live in this part of the jungle. Many have special body coloration and markings to help them hide from their enemies.

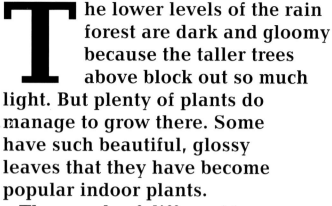

Many understory trees, like this **jackfruit,** have fruits that grow on the trunk, not on branches. Animals are sure to notice these fruits and eat them, thus dispersing the trees' seeds.

Its spotted body keeps the **leaf-tailed gecko** well hidden as it lies pressed almost flat on the bark of a tree or branch.

GUESS WHAT?...

The female marsupial frog uses a tiny skin pouch on her back as a nursery.

The frog lays about 200 eggs and then, with the help of her mate, rolls them into the pouch. A few weeks later, she slits open the pouch with her toe and lets the young tadpoles swim out into a pond.

Lichens and other tiny plants grow on the back of this **weevil,** a type of beetle. They keep the weevil hidden from enemies as it rests on tree trunks.

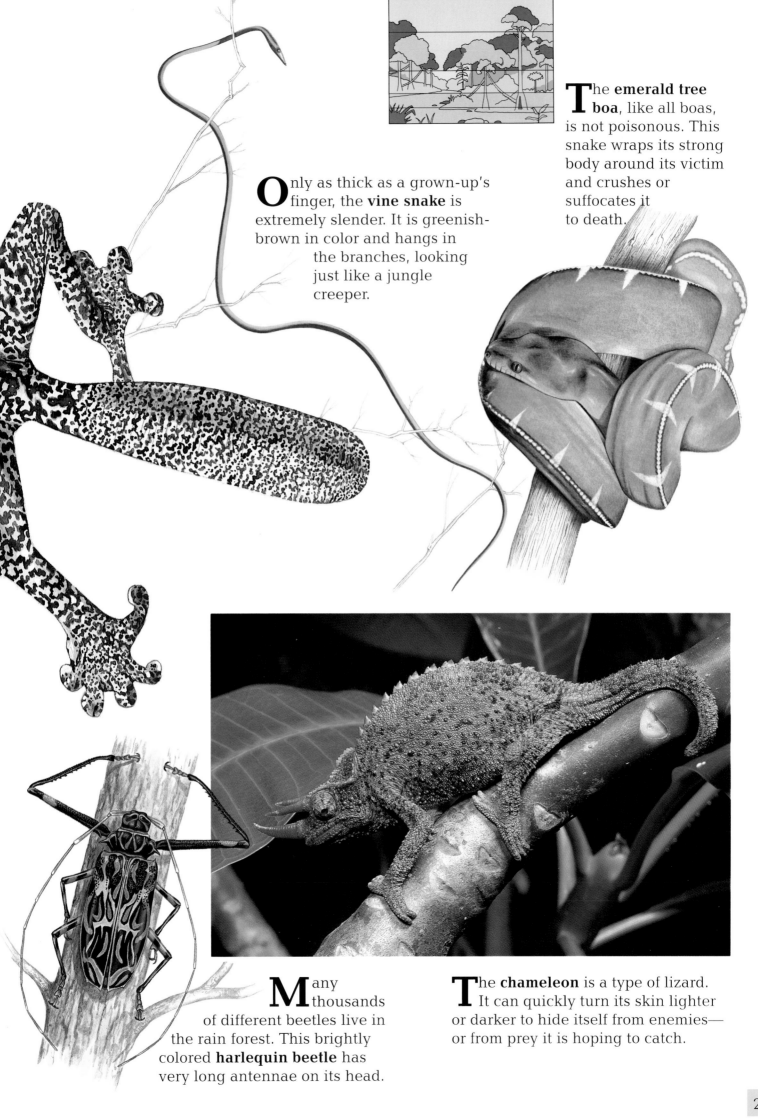

Only as thick as a grown-up's finger, the **vine snake** is extremely slender. It is greenish-brown in color and hangs in the branches, looking just like a jungle creeper.

The **emerald tree boa**, like all boas, is not poisonous. This snake wraps its strong body around its victim and crushes or suffocates it to death.

Many thousands of different beetles live in the rain forest. This brightly colored **harlequin beetle** has very long antennae on its head.

The **chameleon** is a type of lizard. It can quickly turn its skin lighter or darker to hide itself from enemies— or from prey it is hoping to catch.

The dark forest floor

Little sunlight can squeeze through the mass of leaves and branches to the rain forest floor. The ground beneath the towering trees and creepers is so dark that few plants can grow here. But rotting branches and the dead leaves that fall from the trees are home for thousands of ants, termites, and other small creatures.

Gorillas live in groups of up to twenty. They spend most of their lives on the ground but climb into the lower branches to find leaves and fruits to eat.

Elephants use their long, sensitive trunks for feeding, drinking, and even fighting. This is an **Asian elephant**—it has smaller ears and a more humped back than its African relative.

The **okapi** feeds on leaves with the help of a tongue that is so long it can also be used to clean its eyes and eyelids.

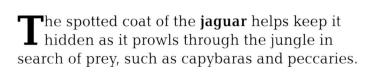

The spotted coat of the **jaguar** helps keep it hidden as it prowls through the jungle in search of prey, such as capybaras and peccaries.

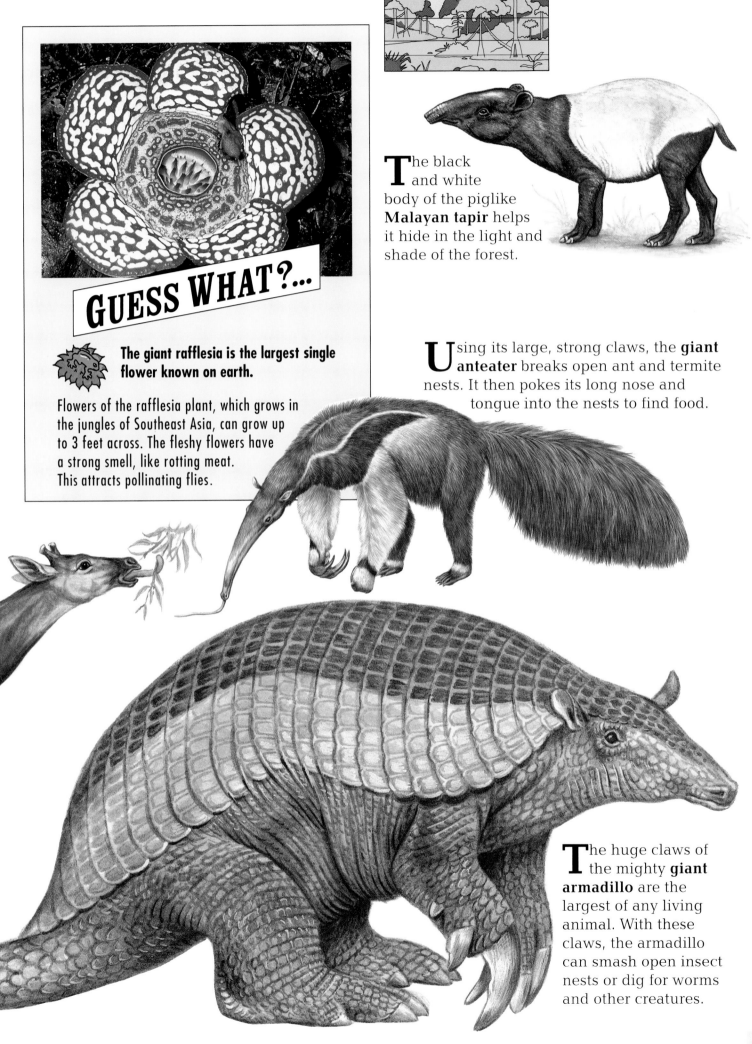

The black and white body of the piglike **Malayan tapir** helps it hide in the light and shade of the forest.

GUESS WHAT?...

The giant rafflesia is the largest single flower known on earth.

Flowers of the rafflesia plant, which grows in the jungles of Southeast Asia, can grow up to 3 feet across. The fleshy flowers have a strong smell, like rotting meat. This attracts pollinating flies.

Using its large, strong claws, the **giant anteater** breaks open ant and termite nests. It then pokes its long nose and tongue into the nests to find food.

The huge claws of the mighty **giant armadillo** are the largest of any living animal. With these claws, the armadillo can smash open insect nests or dig for worms and other creatures.

Many colorful and unusual birds live at this level of the forest. Peacocks, pheasants, and cassowaries search the ground for seeds, fruits, and insects. Others, like the bowerbirds, turn the forest into a display area and build decorative nests, called bowers, to impress likely mates.

But dangerous hunters, such as snakes and spiders, also lurk among the fallen leaves, waiting for the right moment to strike.

Male bowerbirds attract females by building pretty bowers, or nests, from twigs and moss. The male **satin bowerbird** has glossy black feathers, while the female is plainer.

One of the world's most dangerous snakes, the deadly **bushmaster** has poison that can kill even an adult human in a few hours.

The **trapdoor spider** lives in a burrow that it digs with its strong, spiny fangs. At night, the spider waits inside the flaplike door to the burrow until it senses the movement of a nearby insect. It then shoots out and grabs the victim in its poisonous fangs.

Cassowaries are large birds that stand as tall as a man. They cannot fly, but they run fast through the forest. The horny lump on the cassowary's head is called a casque; it may protect the bird's head as the bird moves through dense plants.

The **congo peacock** is a rare bird that was only discovered 50 years ago. Although it lives and feeds on the ground, it probably makes its nest in trees.

GUESS WHAT?...

Leaf-cutter ants grow their own fungus to eat.

Worker leaf-cutter ants cut little pieces of leaves and carry them to their underground "gardens." Fungus grows on the leaves, and the ants feed on it.

25

The jungle river

The rivers and streams that flow through rain forests are home to snakes, crocodiles, and turtles as well as fish. Many other creatures live along the riverbank. The part of the forest next to a river has plenty of light, and plants here grow extra large and thick.

Leaves of the **giant water lily** grow up to 7 feet wide—an adult human could lie down on one! The creamy-colored flowers open at night, when they have a strong smell.

Making a daring swoop within an inch of the water, the **fisherman bat** dips its sharp claws in to seize a fish. It then scoops its catch into its mouth. The bat also catches insects in the air.

The **anaconda** is the heaviest snake in the world. It lies in the water, waiting to grab birds and animals that come to the riverbank to drink.

The **hoatzin** is a poor flier and flaps clumsily as it moves around feeding on the tough leaves of riverside plants. It always makes its nest overhanging the river. To escape from enemies, hoatzin chicks simply drop into the water.

A school of red piranhas can eat a whole cow or other large animal in just a few minutes.

The razor-sharp, pointed teeth of the red piranha can cut through the flesh, and even bone, of its prey with ease. These fish hunt in huge shoals, or schools.

GUESS WHAT?...

The **matamata** turtle has a very bumpy shell and a flat, almost triangular head. It catches fish by lying in the water with its large mouth open. A rush of water—and food— flows down its throat.

Capybaras are the world's largest rodents. They weigh 100 pounds!

A type of crocodile, the **spectacled caiman** is a powerful hunter. It grabs animals that come to the river to drink and holds them underwater until they drown.

Where are the deserts?

Deserts are found in those parts of the world where it is always very dry. So little rain falls on the sandy or rocky ground that few plants can grow. Around the true deserts are areas called semidesert. These places have a little more rainfall. More plants grow there and more kinds of animals can survive.

NORTH AMERICA

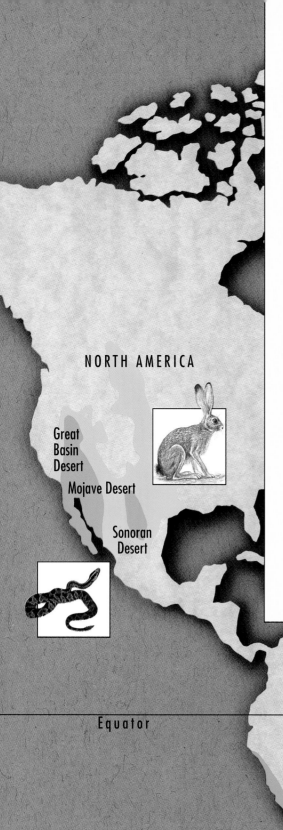

Great Basin Desert

Mojave Desert

Sonoran Desert

Equator

SOUTH AMERICA

Peruvian Desert

Atacama Desert

Patagonian Desert

Sahara Desert

Namib Desert

Desert

Semidesert

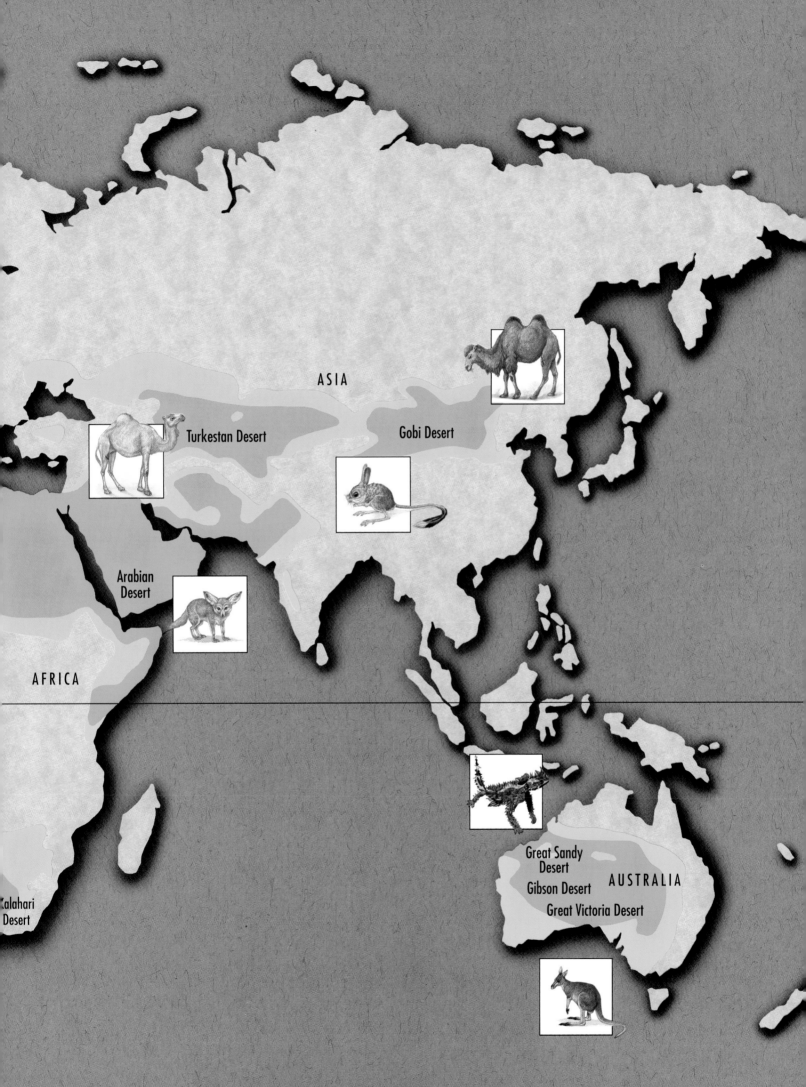

ASIA

Turkestan Desert

Gobi Desert

Arabian
Desert

AFRICA

Kalahari
Desert

Great Sandy
Desert

Gibson Desert

Great Victoria Desert

AUSTRALIA

Living in the desert

Deserts may be hard places to live in, but they are certainly not empty. Many animals and plants survive despite the harsh conditions. Deserts near the equator are hot during the day all year round. But deserts farther away from the equator, such as the Gobi Desert in Asia, are bitterly cold in winter.

Life with no water

The **addax** never seems to drink. It gets all the water it needs from the plants it eats. The addax is particularly good at finding patches of desert plants that spring up after a sudden shower.

Plants and animals need water to stay alive. And finding enough water in the desert is life's biggest problem. Some desert plants have very long roots that spread out to find water. Many desert animals can live for days without actually drinking. They can get enough water from their food.

The male **sand grouse** flies to a water hole, often traveling a long way to find one. He wades in, and special feathers on his breast soak up water like a sponge. He then flies back to the nest where thirsty chicks suck water from his feathers.

Folds of skin in the **chuckwalla** lizard's sides contain special glands in which liquid can be stored. This stored liquid can keep the lizard alive through a long dry season.

GUESS WHAT?...

The darkling beetle survives in the desert by drinking dew.

This beetle lives in the Namib Desert, on the coast of southern Africa. It hardly ever rains there, but in the mornings fog rolls in from the sea, leaving dew on the beetle's body. The beetle then stands on its head and drinks the drops of dew that roll down its back.

Like many desert animals, the Australian **mulgara** has very concentrated urine that helps it retain as much water as possible. The mulgara rarely drinks but gets liquid from the juicy insects and lizards it eats.

When it does rain in the desert, cacti, such as this **organ-pipe cactus**, store up as much water as possible in their large, fleshy stems. This storage system helps the plants stay alive during long dry periods.

A **dromedary camel** can go for days, even weeks, without drinking. But when it does find water, it can drink up to 27 gallons in a few minutes.

Desert **hedgehogs** get moisture from food such as birds' eggs. They also eat deadly scorpions—but only after nipping off the stingers.

Keeping cool and safe

When danger threatens, the desert does not have many hiding places. Instead, desert creatures have found other ways of keeping safe. Many are sandy colored, almost matching their surroundings, and so it is hard for hunting animals to see them. Insects and other small creatures hide underground in the sand.

With little shelter it is easy for animals to get too hot. Many have pale-colored bodies that reflect the sun—dark colors absorb more heat.

Desert larks have dark or light brown feathers, depending on the color of the rocks or sand where they live. This helps them hide from enemies, such as desert cats and foxes.

The pale feathers of the **cream-colored courser** blend with the color of the desert sands and help keep it hidden. This bird usually runs rather than flies, grabbing insects in its sharp beak.

The big ears of the **rabbit-eared bandicoot** help it stay cool. Its ears give off heat—just like a radiator. This bandicoot digs up insects to eat with its strong claws.

There is little shelter from the sun in the sandy desert where the **oryx** lives. A special blood-flow system keeps the blood in the oryx's head cool so its brain does not overheat.

Trees need to keep cool too. **Eucalyptus trees** have white bark that reflects the sun and so keeps the trees from getting too hot.

Like the bandicoot, the **fennec fox** has big ears that keep it cool. These ears also pick up the slightest sound, helping the fox find prey.

The desert sandfish is really a lizard, but it does "swim" through the sand. This little creature burrows into the sand and wriggles along so fast that it almost seems to swim along. Its sandy color helps keep it hidden from enemies as it hunts for beetles and other insects to eat.

GUESS WHAT?...

Fast movers

Soft, shifting sand can make it difficult to get about quickly. But many desert animals have special ways of moving fast. Some snakes and lizards wriggle along, almost as though they are swimming through the sand. Many desert birds have long, slender toes to help spread their weight on the sandy soil. Other desert-living creatures, like the pronghorn, are perfectly designed for fast running on the flat, open land.

The **sand cat** has thick fur, even on the soles of its feet. This helps it move quickly on the sand, protecting it from the heat.

A trail of parallel marks in the sand is the sign of the **sidewinder.** This snake moves by throwing its body into two loops that it then pushes against the ground to move sideways.

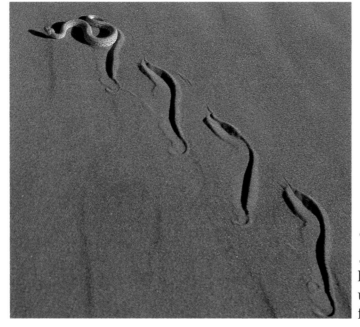

Even when only a few days old, the **pronghorn** can run faster than an adult human. And a fully grown pronghorn can keep up a speed of about 30 miles an hour to escape from its enemies.

The **ostrich**, the largest bird in the world, cannot fly but it is a fast runner. It can race along at speeds of up to 45 miles an hour.

Second only to the ostrich in size, the **emu** is also a speedy bird. It races across the Australian desert in search of food such as berries, grass, and insects.

The webbed feet of this little **gecko** act like snowshoes, helping it move swiftly over the soft sand. The gecko's long legs keep its body well above the baking-hot ground.

GUESS WHAT?...

The greater roadrunner can fly but usually runs very fast after its prey.

Although only 20 inches long, this bird can run at a speed of 12 miles an hour. An expert at catching snakes, the roadrunner grabs its victim just behind the head to avoid getting bitten. It also eats mice, lizards, and spiders.

Hoppers and jumpers

Bounding and hopping movements are well suited to the wide-open spaces of the desert, where there are few trees and bushes to get in an animal's way. Some tiny creatures such as gerbils, jerboas, and kangaroo rats move just like miniature kangaroos—they hop on their two strong back legs instead of running on four legs. Most of these animals have a long tail that helps them keep their balance.

The **black-tailed jackrabbit** can hop along on its long back legs as well as run fast on all fours. It can move at more than 35 miles an hour for short periods.

The **large North African gerbil's** long back legs and feet help it bound along and also keep its body well off the burning sand.

Some wallabies live in forests, but the **spectacled hare-wallaby** spends its life in the Australian desert. It eats the few tough, spiny plants that grow there.

The back legs of the **great jerboa**—an excellent jumper—are at least four times the size of its front legs. It eats seeds and insects, which it finds by combing through the sand with the long claws on its front feet.

Desert kangaroo rats sleep by day and come out at night to find seeds and insects to eat. Like hamsters, they have cheek pouches in which they carry food.

GUESS WHAT?...

Although a red kangaroo is bigger than a grown-up human, its baby is only an inch long at birth.

The female kangaroo carries this tiny baby in the pouch at the front of her body as she bounds along on strong back legs.

The little **grasshopper mouse** catches scorpions and other insects to eat but may sometimes attack other mice.

Burrowers

Deserts may seem empty, but many creatures spend much of their lives hidden in cool, dark burrows just below the surface. Even a few inches down, temperatures are lower and the air a little more moist—a welcome relief from the dry heat of the daytime sun. Once in its burrow, the animal is also safe from desert cats, hawks, and other hunters.

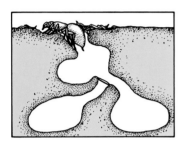

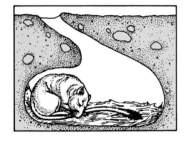

Kangaroo rats and spiders are among the many creatures that live in underground burrows in the desert.

The little **kowari** is a marsupial—it has a pouch like a kangaroo. It lives in burrows, alone or in small groups, and comes out at night to hunt for lizards and insects to eat.

Great gerbils live in the Gobi Desert, where winters are cold. In summer, the gerbils build up stores of plant food in their burrows to help them survive the winter.

Even snakes live in burrows. The **burrowing viper** digs into the soil with its strong snout and usually comes out only at night. It eats small creatures such as lizards, which it kills with its poisonous bite.

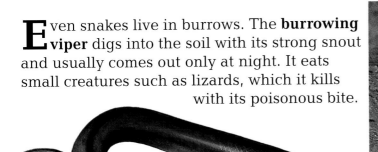

Burrowing owls lay their eggs in burrows, often those left by other animals. But they can also dig their own burrows, using their strong beaks as well as their long legs.

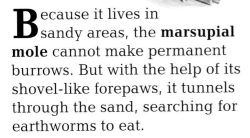

Because it lives in sandy areas, the **marsupial mole** cannot make permanent burrows. But with the help of its shovel-like forepaws, it tunnels through the sand, searching for earthworms to eat.

Spadefoot toads live in burrows, but when the rare rains do come, the toads come out to lay their eggs in rainwater pools.

GUESS WHAT?...

These honeypot ants are living storage pots.

Special workers in a honeypot ant colony are filled with food by other ants until they can hardly move. They then hang upside down in the ants' underground nest until a time of food shortage. Then their stores are used by the whole colony.

Poisoners and stingers

Some of the most poisonous of all creatures live in the desert. There are scorpions, spiders, snakes—and even a poisonous lizard. These creatures use their venomous bites and stings to kill their prey. Food can be hard to find in the desert, and it is useful to be able to kill a victim quickly before it has a chance to escape. A desert animal may also use its poison to defend itself against enemies.

The **diamondback rattlesnake** is one of the most dangerous snakes in North America. It kills its prey by injecting deadly poison through its two sharp, hollow fangs.

Black widow spiders live in all warm regions of the world as well as in deserts. They eat insects such as flies and beetles, and even other spiders, which they catch in their sticky webs.

Saw-scaled adders kill more people than any other snake. But they only bite people in self-defense. Normally the snakes hunt mice, lizards, and insects.

GUESS WHAT?...

The Sahara Desert scorpion has poison so strong that it has been known to kill people.

The scorpion's stinger is at the end of its tail. The scorpion grabs its victim in its pincers, then curves the stinger over its back to deliver the poison.

It may look fierce, but the **red-kneed tarantula** is harmless to humans. It eats insects and small creatures such as lizards, which it kills with its poisonous bite.

Brilliant **red velvet mites** are highly poisonous. Although only a fraction of an inch long, they have even been known to kill mice.

The brightly colored **gila monster** is one of only two poisonous lizards in the world. It kills its prey with a venomous bite. It stores fat in its stumpy tail and lives on this when food is scarce.

Desert hunters

Although some animals manage to survive on desert plants and seeds, many live by hunting and eating other animals. There are several species of cats in the desert, as well as foxes, hyenas, and hunting birds. Most of these hunters can run or fly swiftly and have sharp teeth or claws for killing prey.

Like all vultures, the **lappet-faced vulture** is a scavenger. It searches for dead animals to eat, or finishes off prey that other hunters have killed.

A fierce hunter, the **red-tailed hawk** watches for rabbits and lizards from a perch on a high branch or cactus. It also chases other birds in flight.

The long-legged **caracal** moves fast to pounce on creatures such as lizards, mice, and young antelope. It also climbs trees or leaps into the air to catch birds.

44

Teamwork is the secret of the meerkats' success. Some go hunting while others keep guard or care for the young.

The meerkat is a type of mongoose and lives in family groups of ten to thirty animals. Each meerkat in the group has its own duties. Sentries watch for birds of prey—their main enemies—while other meerkats hunt for small creatures such as lizards, birds, and even snakes.

A small, slender fox with large ears, the **kit fox** hunts at night. It searches for lizards, mice, and other small creatures.

Whether hunting alone or in packs, **dingoes** often travel many miles across the desert in search of food. They are relatives of the domestic dogs first brought to Australia thousands of years ago.

Self-defense

Heat and lack of water are not the only difficulties in the lives of desert animals. They also have to protect themselves against the prowling predators that try to catch them. There are few places to hide, so many desert creatures have other ways of keeping safe. Some, such as the skunk, smell so bad that they put off any would-be hunter. Others are too spiny to eat.

The bright colors of many desert animals, like lizards, also serve as a warning for enemies to stay clear.

The huge **Gould's monitor lizard** is up to 5 feet long—probably bigger than you. It makes itself look fiercer by standing up on its hind legs to threaten its enemies. This Australian lizard hunts for birds, insects, and even other lizards.

The **barrel cactus** is well suited to desert life. It can store water inside its rounded shape to keep itself alive during long dry periods. And its spiny leaves protect it from plant-eating animals.

The thorny devil, a type of lizard that lives in the Australian desert, is as spiny as a cactus plant.

Few animals would dare to attack this creature, even though it is slow-moving and easy to catch. Its body bristles with large, sharp spines from its head to the tip of its tail. Even newly hatched baby thorny devils are covered with spines.

Cactus wrens find their food on the ground but nest on spiny cactus plants to keep their eggs safe from hunters.

The **pancake tortoise** has a very soft, flat shell. When in danger, it hides in a rock crevice. It then puffs up its body by breathing in lots of air so that it becomes firmly wedged in the rocks.

Like all skunks, the **spotted skunk** defends itself from enemies by squirting them with a strong-smelling liquid. This comes from glands under the skunk's tail and smells so bad that it makes it hard for the victim to breathe.

Prickly pear cacti are among the spiniest of all desert plants and almost impossible for animals to eat. These spines are, in fact, very tiny leaves.

After dark

In the burning heat of the day it is too hot for most creatures to move. They would risk overheating and losing too much precious moisture. Instead, they remain completely still in whatever shade they can find by rocks, bushes, or cactus plants. Smaller creatures hide under stones or burrow into the soil.

When dusk falls, these creatures wake up and get busy finding food in the cool of the evening hours.

Its keen senses of hearing and smell help the **small-spotted genet** track down prey such as mice and lizards at night.

The **poorwill** hunts moths and other insects on or near the ground at night.

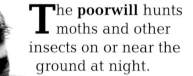

In the heat of the day the **African ass** rests in the shade—if it can find any. At dusk it wanders around searching for grass and other plants in the semidesert where it lives.

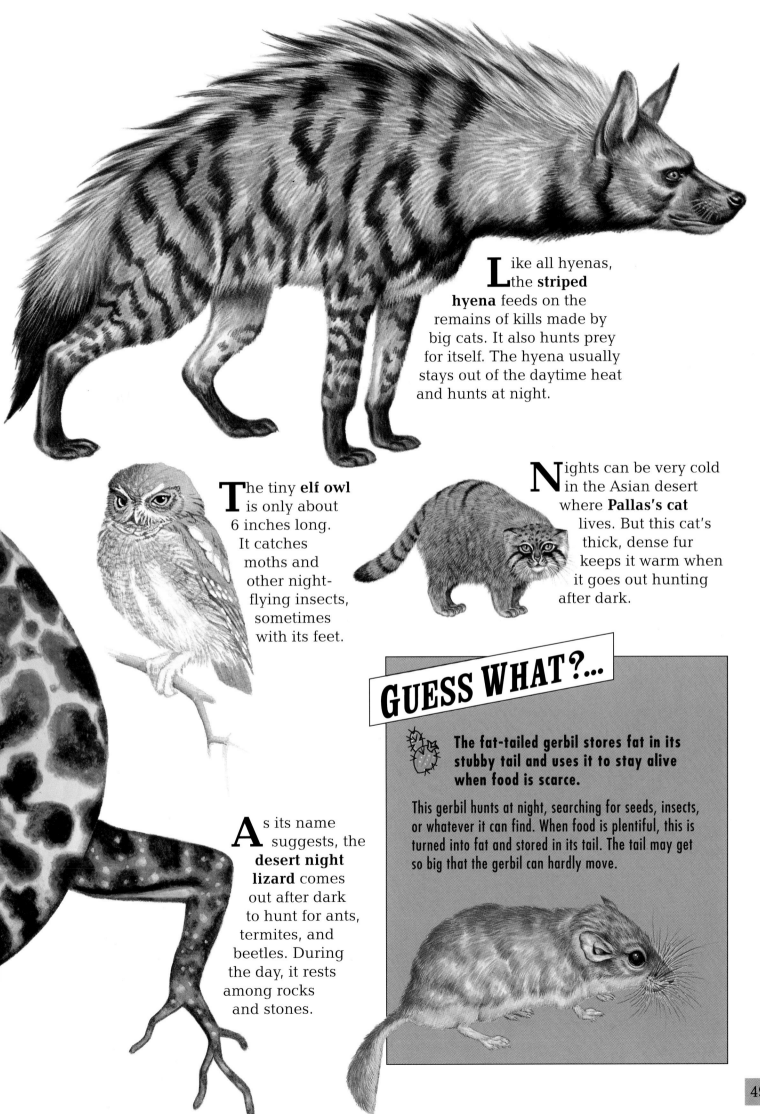

Like all hyenas, the **striped hyena** feeds on the remains of kills made by big cats. It also hunts prey for itself. The hyena usually stays out of the daytime heat and hunts at night.

The tiny **elf owl** is only about 6 inches long. It catches moths and other night-flying insects, sometimes with its feet.

Nights can be very cold in the Asian desert where **Pallas's cat** lives. But this cat's thick, dense fur keeps it warm when it goes out hunting after dark.

GUESS WHAT?...

The fat-tailed gerbil stores fat in its stubby tail and uses it to stay alive when food is scarce.

This gerbil hunts at night, searching for seeds, insects, or whatever it can find. When food is plentiful, this is turned into fat and stored in its tail. The tail may get so big that the gerbil can hardly move.

As its name suggests, the **desert night lizard** comes out after dark to hunt for ants, termites, and beetles. During the day, it rests among rocks and stones.

49

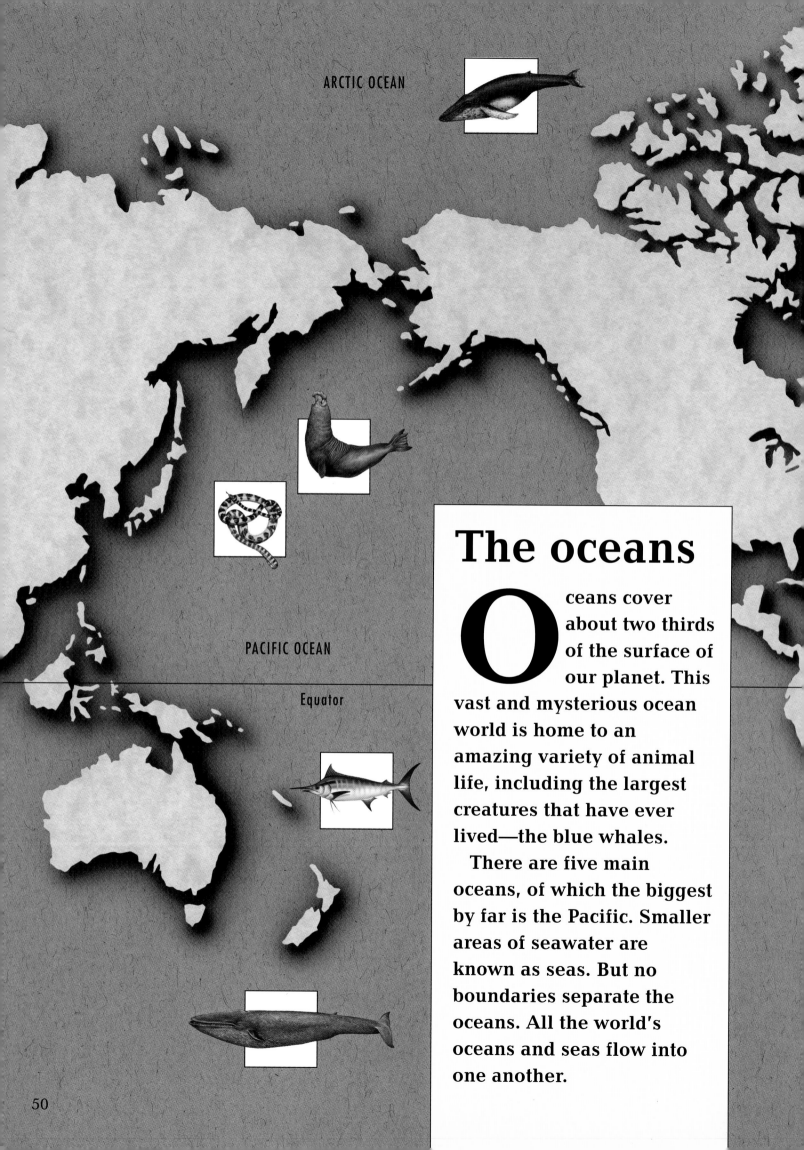

ARCTIC OCEAN

PACIFIC OCEAN

Equator

The oceans

Oceans cover about two thirds of the surface of our planet. This vast and mysterious ocean world is home to an amazing variety of animal life, including the largest creatures that have ever lived—the blue whales.

There are five main oceans, of which the biggest by far is the Pacific. Smaller areas of seawater are known as seas. But no boundaries separate the oceans. All the world's oceans and seas flow into one another.

ADRIATIC
SEA

BLACK SEA

MEDITERRANEAN SEA

RED
SEA

ATLANTIC OCEAN

CARIBBEAN SEA

INDIAN OCEAN

ANTARCTIC OCEAN

51

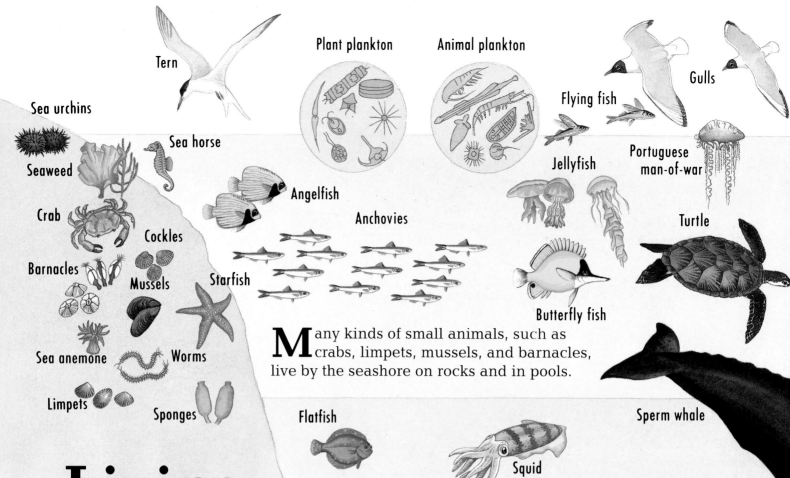

Tern

Plant plankton

Animal plankton

Gulls

Flying fish

Sea urchins

Sea horse

Seaweed

Angelfish

Anchovies

Jellyfish

Portuguese man-of-war

Crab

Turtle

Cockles

Barnacles

Mussels

Starfish

Sea anemone

Worms

Butterfly fish

Limpets

Sponges

Many kinds of small animals, such as crabs, limpets, mussels, and barnacles, live by the seashore on rocks and in pools.

Flatfish

Sperm whale

Living in the ocean

Scallops

Squid

Some of the fish that live in the gloomy midwaters of the ocean have built-in "lights" on their bodies. These lights help the fish find food—and each other.

Lanternfish

Not only fish live in the sea—whales, seals, turtles, shellfish, starfish, crabs, jellyfish, and many other creatures live there too. Some sea animals move just by floating in the ocean currents. Others crawl on the seabed or swim through the water, using their fins and flippers.

The ocean can be divided into different layers, from the sunlit surface waters to the darkest depths. This picture shows some of the animals that live in each layer. In reality, of course, all of these creatures would not be found together.

In the dark waters many hundreds of feet below the surface of the ocean, there is little food. Many deep-sea fish have extra-large mouths so they can easily catch any prey they do find.

Sea lilies

Gannet

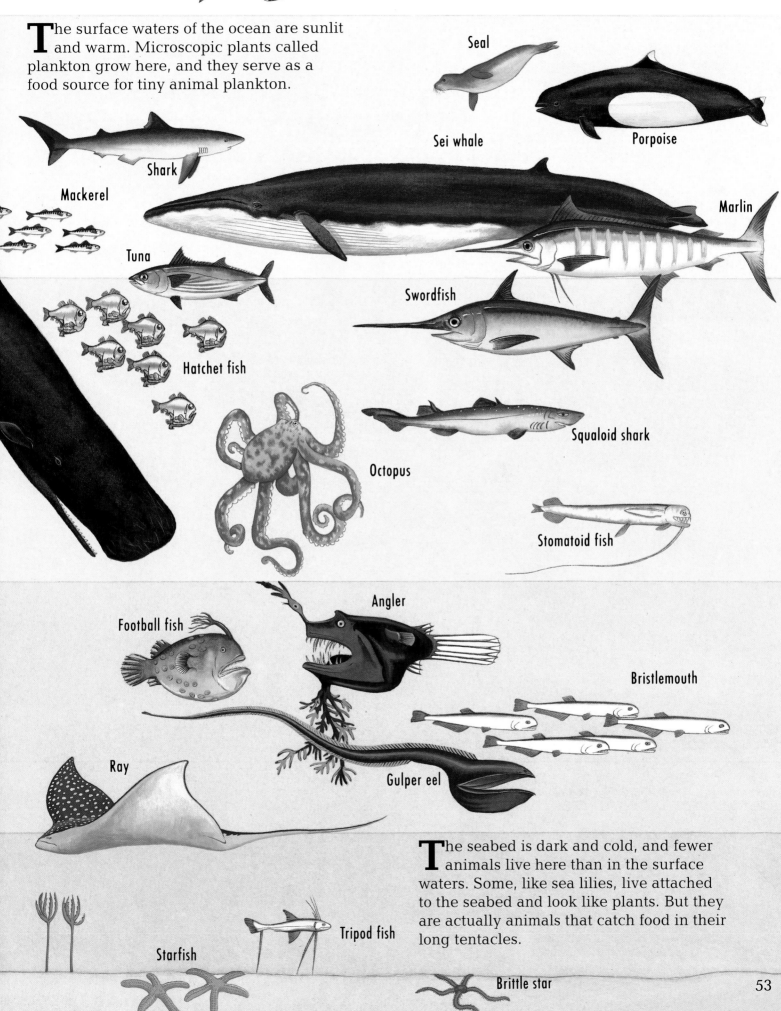

The surface waters of the ocean are sunlit and warm. Microscopic plants called plankton grow here, and they serve as a food source for tiny animal plankton.

Seal

Sei whale

Porpoise

Shark

Mackerel

Marlin

Tuna

Swordfish

Hatchet fish

Octopus

Squaloid shark

Stomatoid fish

Angler

Football fish

Bristlemouth

Ray

Gulper eel

The seabed is dark and cold, and fewer animals live here than in the surface waters. Some, like sea lilies, live attached to the seabed and look like plants. But they are actually animals that catch food in their long tentacles.

Starfish

Tripod fish

Brittle star

53

Between the tides

Land and ocean meet at the seashore, where many kinds of animals make their homes. Seabirds soar overhead and nest on the cliffs. Smaller creatures, such as crabs, mussels, and barnacles, cluster on rocks, in pools, or in burrows in the mud and sand.

But life on the shore is not easy. Tides come in and out twice a day, plunging animals underwater some of the time, then exposing them to the hot sun or cold night air.

The **hermit crab** makes its home in the empty shell of a dead snail or other shelled creature. The shell gives this soft-bodied crab extra protection from hungry hunters. As it grows, the hermit crab moves to bigger shells.

Tiny marine plants, called algae, and seaweed are the main food of the **marine iguana**—the only sea-living lizard. When not in the water, it basks on rocks on the seashore.

Wrasse—a fish with a beaklike mouth for nibbling food off rocks.

The five-armed starfish moves about on hundreds of tiny feet under each of its arms.

These are some animals and plants that live on a rocky shoreline. Those at the bottom of the shore spend most of their lives underwater, while those at the top have to survive long periods out of water.

Lobster

Different species of gulls, like this **black-headed gull**, live around ocean shores. While gulls seldom dive for fish, they do steal eggs, hunt young birds and other creatures, and even feed on garbage heaps.

The **common tern** catches fish to eat. Watching for prey, the tern hovers over the surface of the sea. When it sees something, it dives down and grabs the fish in its beak.

Barnacles

Mussels firmly attached to rocks

Whelk shell

Limpets

Winkles

Red seaweed

Crab

Sea urchin

Living whelk

Prawn feeding in a rock pool

Sea anemones with feeding tentacles stretched out

Green seaweed

Ways of feeding

Nearly everything that lives in the ocean is food for something else. A drop of seawater is full of plants so small that you cannot see them. These are known as plant plankton. Aided by sunlight, they grow in surface waters, where they are eaten by the tiny animal plankton that also fill the ocean.

Some animals, like barnacles, simply strain this tiny plant and animal food from the water through some sort of sieving mechanism in their mouth or body. They are known as filter feeders. Other animals actively chase and hunt their food.

A food chain is a series of feeding links. One animal feeds on another and, in turn, becomes food for yet another animal. This is just one example of a food chain in the ocean. Tiny animal plankton feed on plant plankton. Animal plankton are hunted by small fish, like anchovies. Cod and other larger fish hunt the small fish, but may themselves be devoured by the mighty shark.

With its five strong arms, a **starfish** can pull a shellfish's shell apart, just enough to be able to eat the soft animal inside.

Barnacles live firmly stuck to rocks, floating logs, and even whales. They feed when covered by the sea. The shell opens at the top, and the barnacle pushes out its feathery limbs to trap tiny pieces of food.

GUESS WHAT?...

The sea otter is one of the very few animals that uses a tool to help it get food.

An expert diver, the sea otter finds such food as clams and sea urchins on the seabed. These creatures have very hard shells, but the clever sea otter bangs them against a stone until the shells crack.

Moving in the ocean

Dolphins, such as this **bottle-nosed dolphin**, swim almost exactly like fish—with one difference. They move their tails up and down, not from side to side.

Water is many hundreds of times thicker than air. This makes moving in the sea more difficult than moving on land. A sea animal has to push itself through the water in order to travel.

Fish swim by rhythmically curving their bodies from side to side. At the same time, they beat their flattened fins and tails from side to side to push against the water and propel themselves forward.

The **octopus** can crawl along the seabed on its twisting limbs or shoot water out of its body to force faster movement.

All penguins are expert swimmers. They use their wings as flippers and steer with their webbed feet. This **Galapagos penguin** is the only penguin that lives in warm waters near the equator.

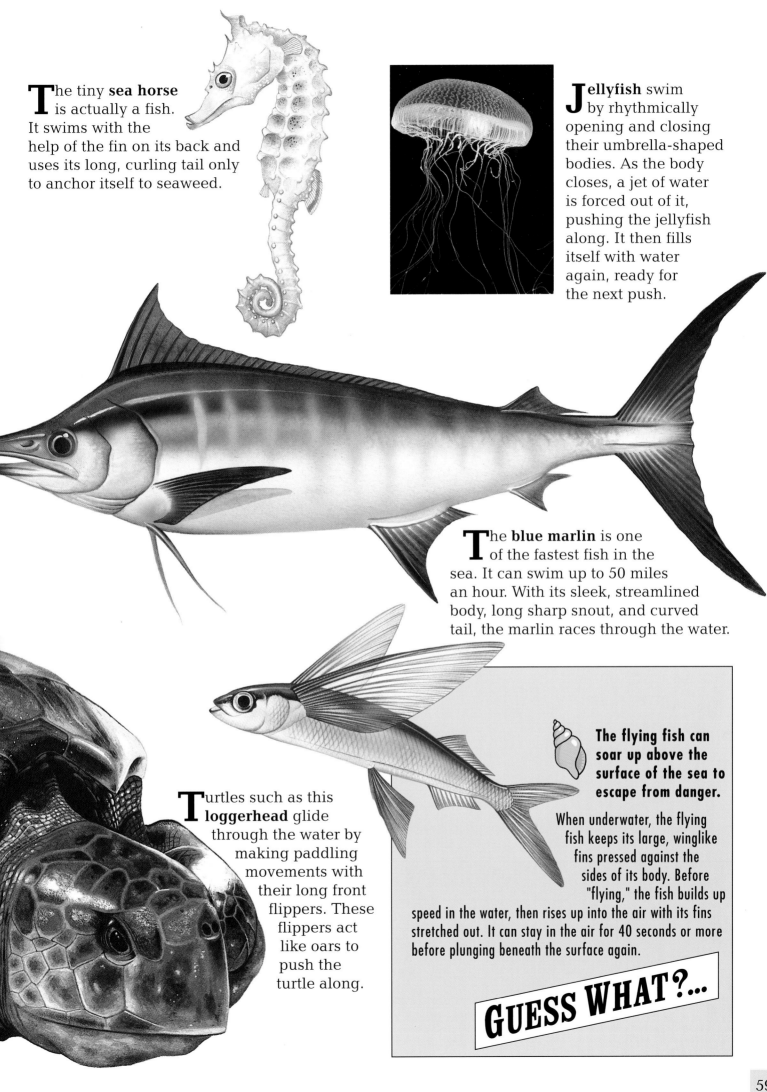

The tiny **sea horse** is actually a fish. It swims with the help of the fin on its back and uses its long, curling tail only to anchor itself to seaweed.

Jellyfish swim by rhythmically opening and closing their umbrella-shaped bodies. As the body closes, a jet of water is forced out of it, pushing the jellyfish along. It then fills itself with water again, ready for the next push.

The **blue marlin** is one of the fastest fish in the sea. It can swim up to 50 miles an hour. With its sleek, streamlined body, long sharp snout, and curved tail, the marlin races through the water.

Turtles such as this **loggerhead** glide through the water by making paddling movements with their long front flippers. These flippers act like oars to push the turtle along.

The flying fish can soar up above the surface of the sea to escape from danger.

When underwater, the flying fish keeps its large, winglike fins pressed against the sides of its body. Before "flying," the fish builds up speed in the water, then rises up into the air with its fins stretched out. It can stay in the air for 40 seconds or more before plunging beneath the surface again.

GUESS WHAT?...

Ocean hunters

Many ocean animals, like land creatures, must hunt to stay alive. Some of these hunters are armed with special weapons, like poisonous fangs, that help them catch their prey. Others, such as sharks and killer whales, are so fast and powerful that there are few animals that can escape them. Just as lions and tigers are on land, sharks and killer whales are top hunters in the sea.

The largest of all crocodiles, the **estuarine crocodile** measures up to 20 feet long—about the length of two cars. It spends most of its life in the sea, hunting for fish and other prey.

Fierce **killer whales** can catch fish, squid, sea lions, and even other whales. They live and hunt in family groups of about forty or more.

GUESS WHAT?...

 The head of the hammerhead shark is stretched out sideways into a T-shape. One eye and one nostril are at each end.

Nobody knows why this shark has such a strange-shaped head. Some people think that the wide space between its eyes and nostrils make its powers of sight and smell extra sensitive.

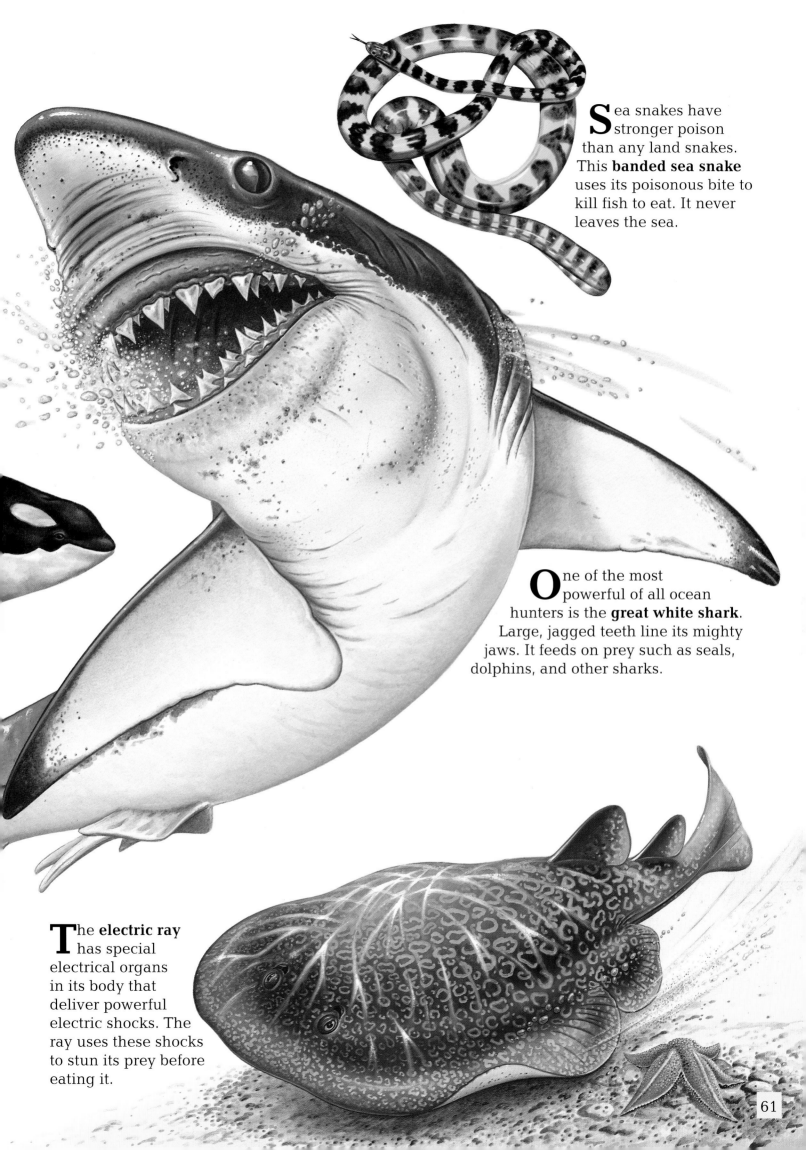

Sea snakes have stronger poison than any land snakes. This **banded sea snake** uses its poisonous bite to kill fish to eat. It never leaves the sea.

One of the most powerful of all ocean hunters is the **great white shark**. Large, jagged teeth line its mighty jaws. It feeds on prey such as seals, dolphins, and other sharks.

The **electric ray** has special electrical organs in its body that deliver powerful electric shocks. The ray uses these shocks to stun its prey before eating it.

Ocean giants

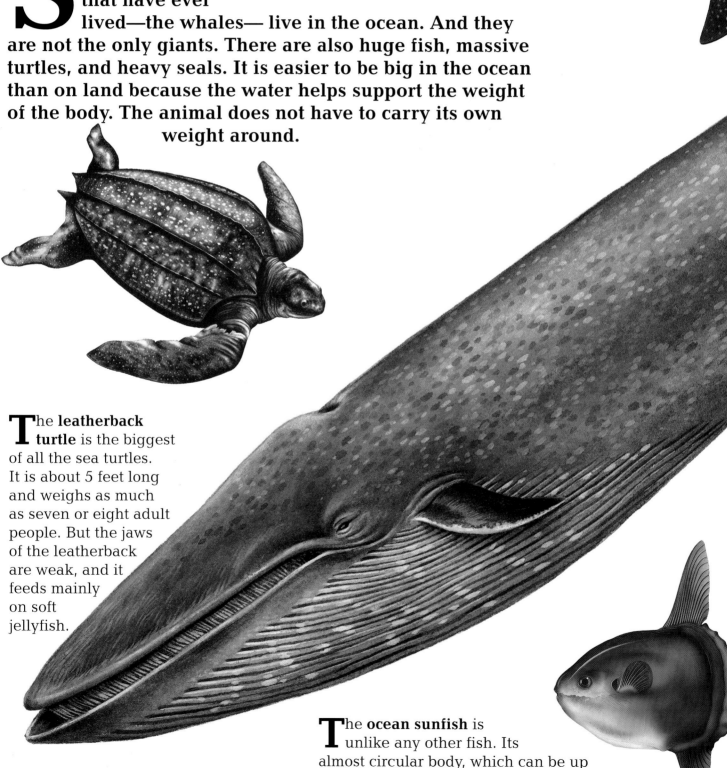

Some of the biggest animals that have ever lived—the whales— live in the ocean. And they are not the only giants. There are also huge fish, massive turtles, and heavy seals. It is easier to be big in the ocean than on land because the water helps support the weight of the body. The animal does not have to carry its own weight around.

The **leatherback turtle** is the biggest of all the sea turtles. It is about 5 feet long and weighs as much as seven or eight adult people. But the jaws of the leatherback are weak, and it feeds mainly on soft jellyfish.

The **ocean sunfish** is unlike any other fish. Its almost circular body, which can be up to 10 feet long, ends in a strange frill-like tail.

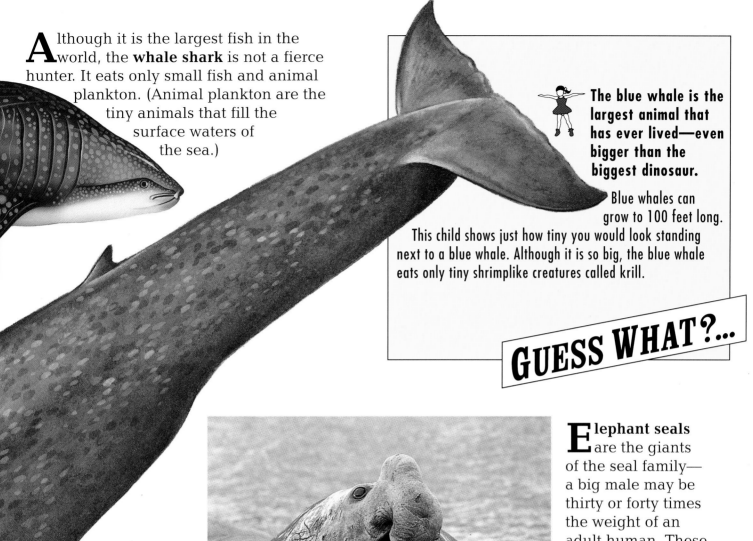

Although it is the largest fish in the world, the **whale shark** is not a fierce hunter. It eats only small fish and animal plankton. (Animal plankton are the tiny animals that fill the surface waters of the sea.)

The blue whale is the largest animal that has ever lived—even bigger than the biggest dinosaur.

Blue whales can grow to 100 feet long. This child shows just how tiny you would look standing next to a blue whale. Although it is so big, the blue whale eats only tiny shrimplike creatures called krill.

GUESS WHAT?...

Elephant seals are the giants of the seal family— a big male may be thirty or forty times the weight of an adult human. These huge males have fierce battles with one another to win territory and mates.

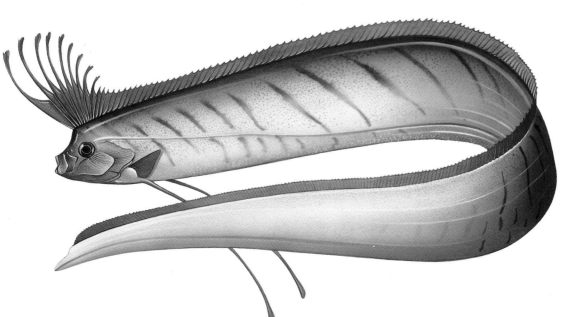

The extraordinary **oarfish** has a ribbonlike body that can be as long as 23 feet. It swims with rippling, snakelike movements. The oarfish has no teeth and usually eats small shrimp.

Diving beneath the waves

The **gannet** soars high above the ocean, searching for fish. Once it spots some prey, it dives into the water at lightning speed, grabs the fish, and brings it to the surface.

Ocean creatures such as seabirds, seals, whales, and dolphins must dive down beneath the surface of the sea to find food. Gannets and pelicans have become expert divers, able to plunge into the water at high speed to grab their meals. Seals and dolphins must surface to breathe, but they can stay underwater to chase their prey for much longer than humans can.

A seal's heart beats more slowly while underwater so that its body uses up less oxygen.

Dall's porpoise, like all porpoises, is actually a small whale. To hunt for fish and squid, it makes dives that last about six minutes.

GUESS WHAT?...

Dolphins can "talk" to one another while swimming underwater.

When dolphins are hunting, they make whistling sounds that seem to help them stay in touch with one another. Sound travels four times more quickly in water than in air, so their messages move fast and far.

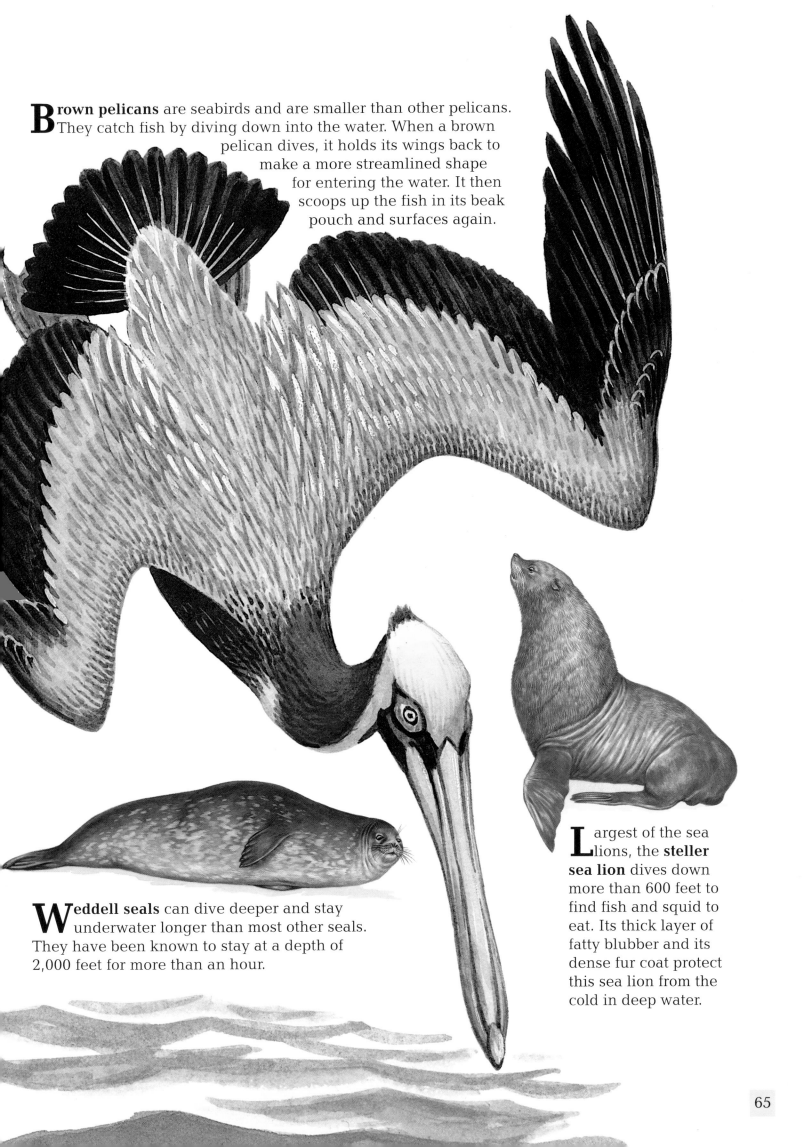

Brown pelicans are seabirds and are smaller than other pelicans. They catch fish by diving down into the water. When a brown pelican dives, it holds its wings back to make a more streamlined shape for entering the water. It then scoops up the fish in its beak pouch and surfaces again.

Largest of the sea lions, the **steller sea lion** dives down more than 600 feet to find fish and squid to eat. Its thick layer of fatty blubber and its dense fur coat protect this sea lion from the cold in deep water.

Weddell seals can dive deeper and stay underwater longer than most other seals. They have been known to stay at a depth of 2,000 feet for more than an hour.

65

Ocean travelers

Whales, fish, and turtles are some of the sea creatures that make long journeys called migrations. These journeys are often between one place where the sea creatures mate and lay their eggs and another place that is rich in food. Seabirds migrate, too, often traveling long distances over the sea. No one knows exactly how these travelers find their way. Some birds seem to navigate by the stars. Swimming migrators may use their sense of taste to tell one current from another.

A shearwater removed from its nest in Britain and taken to the United States returned home, a distance of about 2,800 miles, in just 13 days.

Usually though, the shearwater travels from European North Atlantic coasts, where it lays its eggs, far across the ocean to South America, where it spends the winter months.

GUESS WHAT?...

Most **storm petrels** lay their eggs and raise their young on North Atlantic coasts during the spring and summer. In winter, they fly south to the warmer weather on the coasts of Africa and the Red Sea.

Humpback whales spend summers at the North or South Poles, where there are plenty of small fish and shrimplike krill for food. In winter, the humpbacks migrate to warmer seas near the equator, where females give birth to their young. When the young are big enough to travel, the whales return to polar seas.

Green turtles feed on underwater plants off the coast of South America. But they travel halfway to Africa, to tiny Ascension Island in the Atlantic Ocean, to lay their eggs.

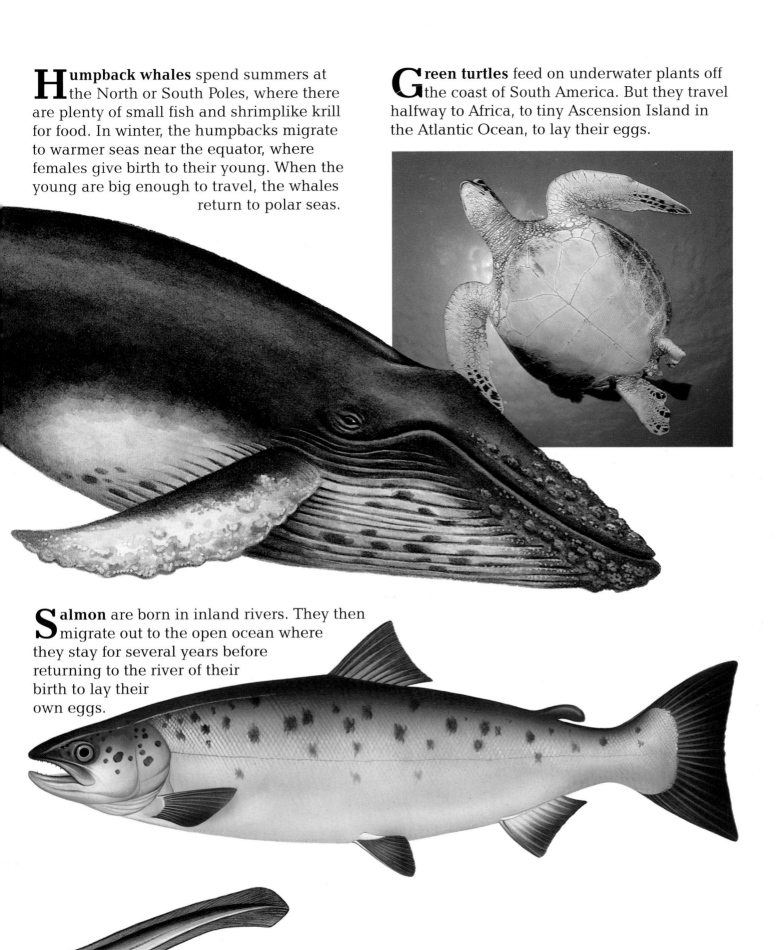

Salmon are born in inland rivers. They then migrate out to the open ocean where they stay for several years before returning to the river of their birth to lay their own eggs.

Eels spend part of their lives in the sea, part in rivers. They lay their eggs in the Sargasso Sea, off the southeast coast of Florida. After hatching, the baby eels drift in surface waters for several years until they reach coastal waters. They swim up into rivers, where they live for several more years while they grow into adults. The full-grown eels then travel all the way back to the Sargasso Sea, where they were born, to lay their eggs. Most only spawn once or twice in a lifetime.

The deepest ocean

Down below the surface waters, the ocean is very dark and very cold. No plants live in these deep waters because there is no sunlight. There are only animals, such as fish and squid, hunting each other. Because it is so dark, many deep-sea fish have their own "living lights."

The **football fish** has its own "fishing rod," tipped with a light-producing organ, on its head. It gobbles up the fish that are attracted to its shining lure.

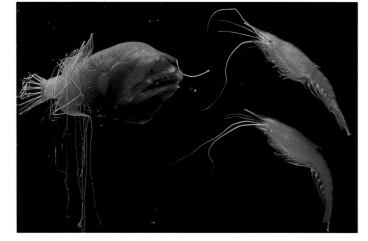

Like many deep-sea fish, the **angler** has a special spine, tipped with a flap of skin, on its head. This spine acts just like a fishing rod. Other creatures, like these shrimp, come to the lure, thinking it is food, and are then snapped up in the angler's large jaws.

The back fin of the **Sloane's viperfish** has one long ray, or spine, that dangles like a fishing lure in front of its head. When prey comes near to look at this lure, the viperfish seizes the prey in its sharp fangs.

The **gulper eel** has a small, thin body but a huge, gaping mouth. It probably swims with its jaws open, swallowing any fish that stray into its mouth.

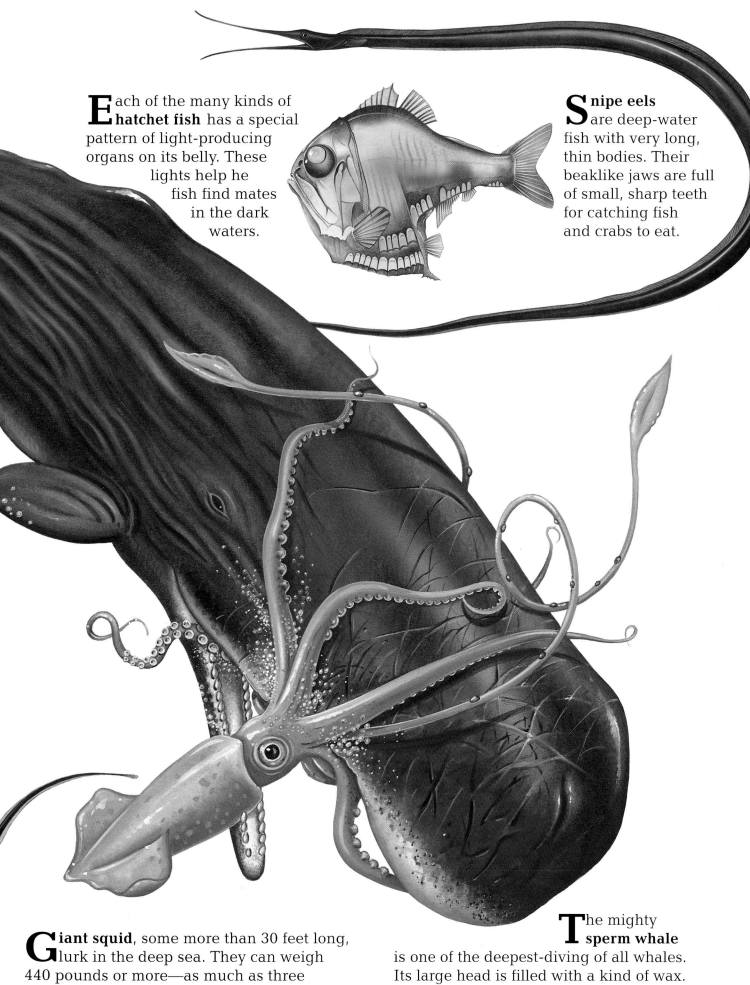

Each of the many kinds of **hatchet fish** has a special pattern of light-producing organs on its belly. These lights help he fish find mates in the dark waters.

Snipe eels are deep-water fish with very long, thin bodies. Their beaklike jaws are full of small, sharp teeth for catching fish and crabs to eat.

Giant squid, some more than 30 feet long, lurk in the deep sea. They can weigh 440 pounds or more—as much as three adults—and their only real enemy is the sperm whale. But the squid do not give up without a struggle. Most sperm whales are covered with marks made by the tentacles of the battling squid.

The mighty sperm whale is one of the deepest-diving of all whales. Its large head is filled with a kind of wax. Some scientists believe that this wax hardens as the whale dives, helping it to go down. As the whale comes back up again, its blood warms and melts the wax, helping to speed the whale's return to the surface.

The coral reef

The amazing underwater world of a coral reef is home to many kinds of brightly colored fish as well as crabs, shellfish, and other creatures. Most coral reefs are in shallow water in tropical areas, such as the Caribbean Sea and the Indian Ocean. This warm, shallow water best suits the coral animals, the small creatures that build the reef.

If in danger, the **clown triggerfish** hides in a crevice in the coral and wedges itself in with a spine on its back.

GUESS WHAT?...

A coral reef is not made of rock, but of the piled-up skeletons of many coral animals.

The coral animals live in large colonies. Like sea anemones, they have tentacles for catching food.

Tentacle

Rocky skeleton

Mouth

An expert hunter, the **great barracuda** catches other fish on the reef with the help of its large mouth, which is studded with sharp teeth.

Like many coral reef fish, the **moorish idol** has bright, bold markings. These may warn other fish that the moorish idol is not good to eat.

A kind of sea horse, the **weedy sea dragon** has many leaflike flaps of skin on its long body. These may help it hide from its enemies, concealing the creature among seaweed.

The **imperial angelfish** feeds on the coral animals themselves. The stripes on the fish's body are believed to confuse a would-be predator. The stripes lead the hunter's eyes toward the tail and away from the easily damaged head area.

The **forceps butterfly fish** has long, pointed jaws that it uses to pick out tiny creatures from the coral reef.

Giant clams are huge shellfish that live among the coral. One clam may weigh more than 400 pounds—as much as three people.

Parrot fish feed on ocean plants called algae, which they scrape from rocks with their beaklike jaws. Parrot fish damage reefs by breaking off pieces of coral as they "graze."

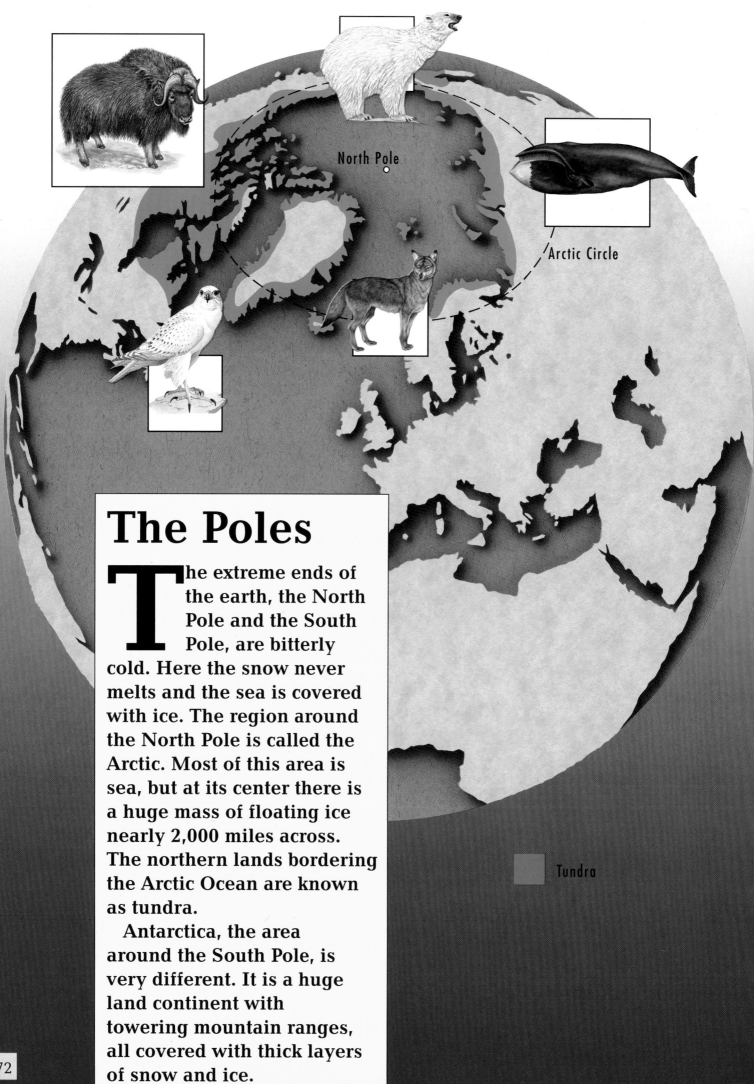

North Pole

Arctic Circle

Tundra

The Poles

The extreme ends of the earth, the North Pole and the South Pole, are bitterly cold. Here the snow never melts and the sea is covered with ice. The region around the North Pole is called the Arctic. Most of this area is sea, but at its center there is a huge mass of floating ice nearly 2,000 miles across. The northern lands bordering the Arctic Ocean are known as tundra.

Antarctica, the area around the South Pole, is very different. It is a huge land continent with towering mountain ranges, all covered with thick layers of snow and ice.

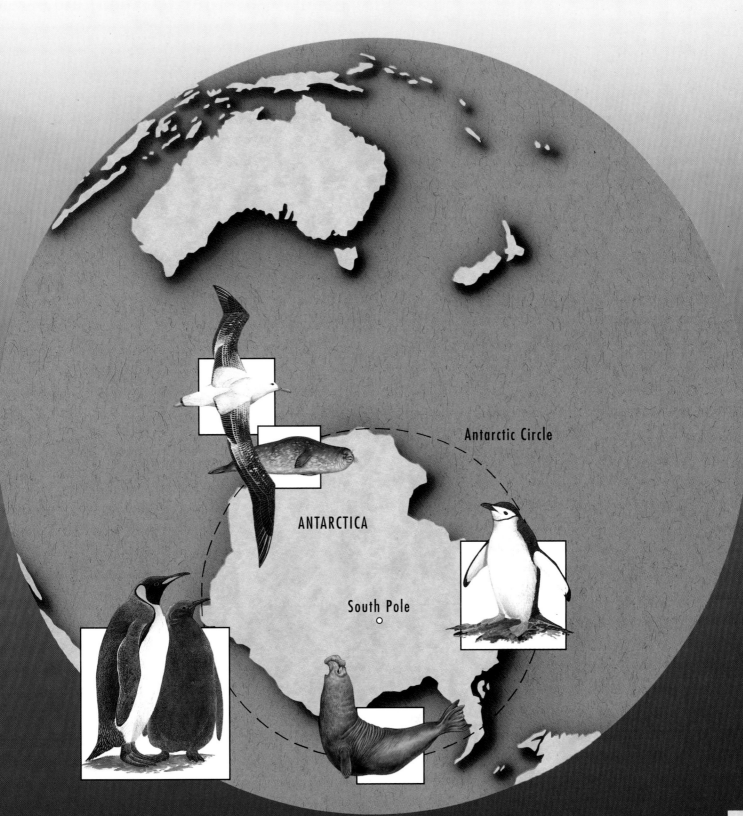

Antarctic Circle

ANTARCTICA

South Pole

Life in the Arctic

On the frozen polar ice cap itself, there are few plants or insects. But animals do manage to live there, catching fish or hunting one another. These animals, such as polar bears and seals, have thick coats of fur or layers of fatty blubber that help protect them from the cold. Many seabirds visit the Arctic, but usually only in the brief summer.

Life in the Antarctic

Antarctica is the **coldest place on earth, with fierce winds and stormy seas. Temperatures there can go as low as –120°F. No land animals live on Antarctica except a few tiny insects** like mites—the biggest of these is only half an inch long. But there is plenty of food in Antarctic seas for birds like penguins and for the many types of seals and whales.

Key

These pictures show some of the animals and birds that live in the Arctic and the Antarctic. In nature, they would not all be seen together. The Arctic tern migrates between both the Arctic and the Antarctic.

1 Snow goose	8 Arctic fox	15 Skua	20 Gentoo penguin
2 Graylag goose	9 Narwhal	16 Fur seal	21 King penguin and young
3 Arctic wolf	10 Puffin	17 Emperor penguin	22 Storm petrel
4 Ermine	11 Ptarmigan	18 Chinstrap penguin	23 Wandering albatross
5 Polar bear	12 Arctic tern	19 Adélie penguin	
6 Harp seal	13 Killer whale		
7 Walrus	14 Elephant seal		

Life on the tundra

The cold, bare lands at the edges of the Arctic Ocean are known as the tundra. No trees survive the fierce winds that blow here, but some small ground-hugging plants grow in the short summer. These plants are food for animals such as lemmings and caribou. Many birds come to the tundra during the Arctic summer, but they fly south again in the harsh winter months.

Key

Some typical tundra animals are shown in this picture. In nature, of course, these animals would not all be seen together.

1 Arctic hare
2 Caribou
3 Tundra swan
4 Gyrfalcon
5 Snow bunting
6 Wolverine
7 Musk oxen
8 Ptarmigan
9 Arctic ground squirrel
10 Lemming
11 Ermine (summer coat)l

Hiding in the snow

In the snowy wastes of the polar regions there are no trees and very few places for animals to hide from their enemies or to lie in wait for prey. The best way to keep out of sight is to blend into the background. That's why so many polar animals and birds have white fur or feathers. This makes them hard to see in the snowy landscape. Imagine how easy it would be to spot a parrot in the Arctic!

In summer, **ptarmigans'** feathers are mottled browns and grays. In winter, all but the tip of their tail feathers turn white.

The white coat of the **Arctic fox** keeps the animal perfectly hidden as it creeps up on lemmings, its main prey. And this coat is also so long and dense that it may be the warmest of any animal fur.

Arctic gyrfalcons are large, powerful birds. They fly close to the ground in search of prey—usually other birds.

Even the **Arctic hare's** feet are covered with thick fur. This helps the hare's feet grip the slippery snow and keeps them warm as well. In summer, when the snows melt on the tundra, the hare's white fur turns brown.

The **ermine**, also known as the shorttail weasel, is almost pure white in winter. But when summer comes to the Arctic tundra, its thick coat turns brown.

Male **snowy owls** have spectacular white feathers, but females have many more dark, barred markings. Unlike most owls, the snowy owl hunts in the daytime, pouncing on lemmings, hares, and other small animals.

GUESS WHAT?...

Probably no animal lives farther north than the polar bear. The tracks of polar bears have been found only a mile or two from the North Pole.

One of the largest of all land hunters, the mighty polar bear prowls the Arctic wilderness, searching for seals, its main prey. It often grabs the seals from their breathing holes in the ice.

Keeping warm

To escape from the bitter cold, the little **snow bunting** sometimes burrows into the snow. This bird nests farther north than any other bird.

Thick coats of fur or feathers keep animals and birds that live in the coldest parts of the world warm. But cold water takes heat from an animal's body faster than air does, so sea-living polar creatures need more protection. They have layers of fatty blubber under their skin that keep them from losing too much body heat in icy seas.

The **eider duck** plucks warm, downy feathers from its breast to cover its eggs in the nest and prevent them from getting cold.

The musk ox's winter coat is longer than that of any other animal. Some of its thick hair is 3 feet long and reaches almost to the ground.

Under the outer coat of the musk ox is a thick layer of underfur that keeps out the cold and wet of the Arctic winter.

GUESS WHAT?...

Penguins, like the **chinstrap penguin**, have two layers of feathers as well as a layer of fatty blubber. The first layer of soft, downy feathers is covered by harder, oily feathers, which keep the penguin waterproof as well as warm.

Elephant seals are the biggest of all seals. A full-grown male can weigh up to 8,000 pounds—more than 40 or 50 humans. Once a year the elephant seal molts: it sheds its skin and hair and grows a sleek new coat.

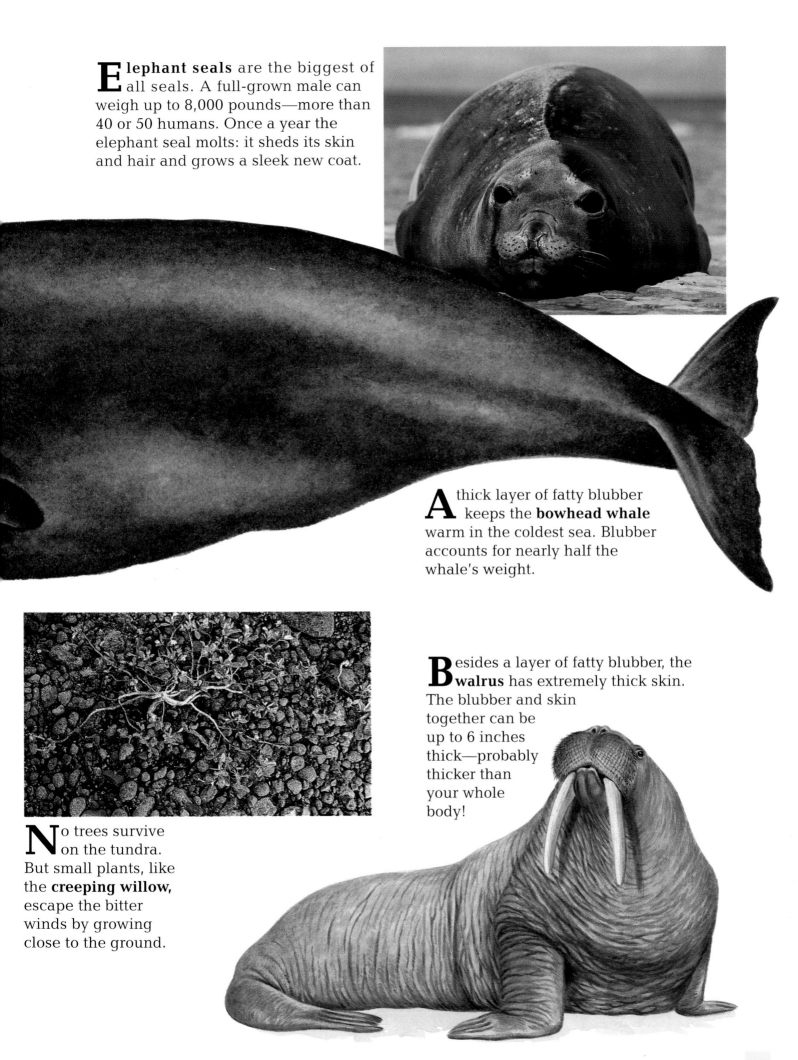

A thick layer of fatty blubber keeps the **bowhead whale** warm in the coldest sea. Blubber accounts for nearly half the whale's weight.

Besides a layer of fatty blubber, the **walrus** has extremely thick skin. The blubber and skin together can be up to 6 inches thick—probably thicker than your whole body!

No trees survive on the tundra. But small plants, like the **creeping willow,** escape the bitter winds by growing close to the ground.

Life on the ice

The icy wastes of the Arctic and the Antarctic do not look like comfortable homes, but some animals manage to live there all year round. There is always plenty of fish, shrimplike krill, and other shellfish for seals and the many types of polar birds to feed on. In the worst of the winter weather, seals spend most of their time in the sea, but in summer they haul themselves out onto the ice to bask in the sun.

The **ivory gull** follows polar bears and picks up the scraps from their meals as well as catching fish. It can run over the ice on its short, stumpy legs.

Gentoo penguins spend much of the winter in the sea, but in spring they trek across land to their breeding places on Antarctica. Penguins cannot fly, and the journey over the ice on foot may take many days.

Crabeater seals move fast over the ice, thrusting themselves forward with their front flippers. They may reach speeds of up to 15 miles an hour. Crabeaters are the most common type of seal in the Antarctic.

When penguins reach a slope, they often lie down on their bellies and "toboggan" over the snow, pushing themselves along with their flippers.

Ringed seals spend winter below the ice, coming to the surface at holes in the ice to breathe.

Under the ice

The seas around the Poles teem with life. Temperatures in polar waters are more constant than land temperatures, and there are some warm currents. The smallest ocean life in the polar waters are the millions of tiny animals known as plankton.

Many kinds of fish also thrive in polar seas. Some of these have a sort of anti-freeze substance inside them that keeps their body fluids from turning to ice.

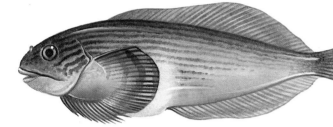

The **striped sea snail** has a little suction disk on its underside. With this, it can attach itself to the seabed or to seaweed.

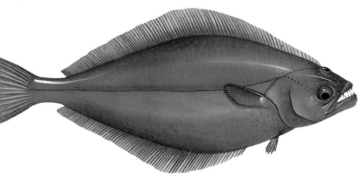

The **Greenland halibut** is a flatfish. Like all flatfishes it has both eyes on the right side of its body. It catches shellfish and squid in its strong, fanglike teeth.

GUESS WHAT?...

 The icefish has blood that is almost transparent, not red like the blood of other creatures.

Icefish are the only creatures that have no oxygen-carrying red blood cells. A small amount of oxygen is carried in their blood, and because the fish are very sluggish, this is enough for their needs.

Skates spend much of their lives on the seabed, where they lie in wait for prey such as fish, crabs, and lobsters. The skate's body is very flat, and it has wide fins that look like wings. When the skate swims, it flaps these fins so it looks almost as if it is flying though the water.

The shrimplike **Antarctic krill** live in huge swarms. There are millions of individuals in a swarm. Each krill is about 3 inches long, including its antennae.

The **Antarctic cod** is well adapted to polar life. These fish have a special substance in their blood that lowers their freezing point and prevents them from turning to ice.

Unlike most fish, the **lumpfish** has no scales. Its rounded body is studded with rows of spiny plates.

Finding food

In the parts of the polar regions that are covered with snow all year round, the sea is the most important source of food for most animals. But on the Arctic tundra, where the snows melt each summer, animals can find food on land. As the ground thaws, new plants grow and flowers open, bringing plenty of leaves and seeds for plant eaters.

Warble flies are among the many insects that fill the air in the tundra summer. Their young, or larvae, live in and feed on the bodies of large animals like caribou.

King penguins dive deep in search of fish and squid. Most dives are down to about 160 feet, but king penguins have been known to plunge as deep as 800 feet—roughly the height of an 80-story building.

Young king penguin

The **puffin** seizes fish from the sea and carries it back to its nest in its large, strong beak. Puffins swim and dive well. Unlike penguins, they can fly.

Wilson's petrel hops and paddles over the surface of the ocean in search of shrimp and other shellfish. It often follows ships, picking up the creatures brought to the surface in the ship's wake.

The **leopard seal** is much slimmer than most seals and has a longer, more flexible neck. Built for speed, the leopard seal is a fierce hunter and snaps up young seals and penguins on the ice and under water.

The little **lemming** scurries along the ground searching for seeds and grass to eat. It will even dig beneath the snow to find food.

Snowy **sheathbills** eat almost anything they can find. They catch fish, seize the eggs and young from other birds' nests, and even visit the garbage cans of Antarctic science stations!

Arctic ground squirrels hibernate through the winter months. In the brief summer, they must eat plenty of roots, leaves, berries, and other plant material to build up their stores of body fat.

Hunters of the north

Great skuas do catch fish, but they also get much of their food by chasing other seabirds and forcing them to give up any food they are carrying.

In the far north, animals that live by hunting must be adaptable, able to take advantage of any food that comes along. Animals such as wolves and wolverines attack creatures larger than themselves, but they will also pounce on a tiny mouse or fill up on berries. In such harsh conditions, animals cannot afford to be too choosy.

The male **narwhal** has a long tusk—actually a huge tooth—but it does not use the tusk for hunting. Some scientists think that the narwhal uses its tusk to battle with rival males for mates and territory.

Brown bears live in tundra areas and northern forests, where they hunt for small animals and fish. Bears will eat almost anything, however, and in late summer they gorge on fruit, nuts, and berries.

The **sable** hunts mice and other small creatures but also gobbles up any insects, nuts, berries, and honey that it can find.

Although a powerful hunter, the **wolverine** has short legs and is not a fast mover. It can catch animals larger than itself that have been slowed by deep snow. Alternatively, it hides and ambushes unsuspecting small animals and birds.

GUESS WHAT?...

Gray wolves are fierce hunters, but they live in close-knit family groups, or packs, and help each other hunt.

Working in groups of eight or more, gray wolves can bring down an animal as large as a musk ox, six or seven times their own weight.

On the tundra, wolves also hunt caribou, following the herds as they migrate in search of food.

The **hooded seal** dives deep to catch fish, such as halibut and haddock. The male hooded seal has a special pouch of skin on its nose. This pouch can be blown up when the animal is alarmed or in danger, and the inflated "hood" then scares away an enemy or rival.

The fierce **killer whale** prowls Arctic coasts in search of fish, squid, seals, birds, and even other whales. Killer whales often swim in groups and hunt together.

Polar travelers

Every fall, herds of **caribou** travel hundreds of miles from the tundra, where they live and breed in summer, to winter feeding areas farther south. Here the caribou feed mainly on lichens, scraping away the snow with their hooves to expose the plants. When spring comes, they return once more to the tundra.

Animals Migrate in order to get the best of two worlds. For many creatures, conditions in the Arctic are good in summer—there is plenty of food, and on the tundra the temperature even creeps above freezing. But at the end of the summer, many flee south to find winter food supplies and escape the cold.

The **golden plover** lays its eggs and rears its young on the tundra. In fall, it flies some 8,000 miles south to South America or to islands in the Pacific where it spends the winter.

In the fall, **gray whales** begin the 13,000-mile journey south to breeding areas in the Pacific Ocean— one of the longest migrations of any animal.

90

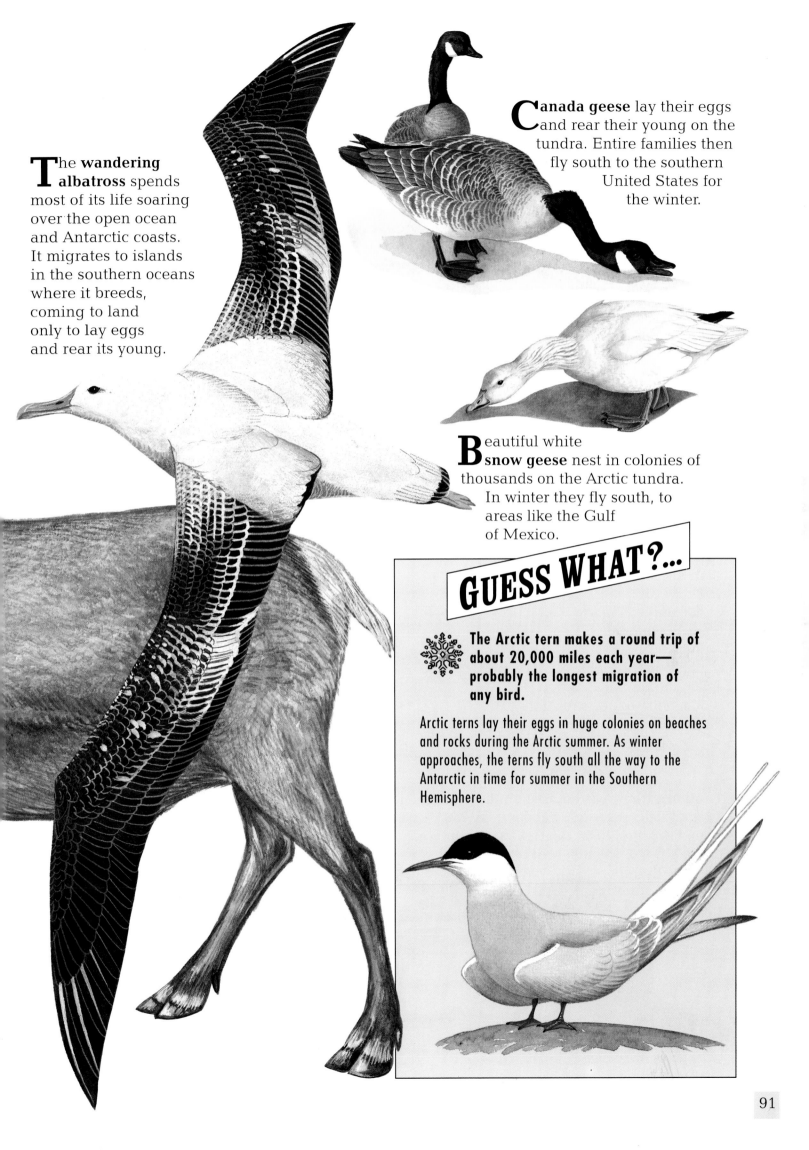

The **wandering albatross** spends most of its life soaring over the open ocean and Antarctic coasts. It migrates to islands in the southern oceans where it breeds, coming to land only to lay eggs and rear its young.

Canada geese lay their eggs and rear their young on the tundra. Entire families then fly south to the southern United States for the winter.

Beautiful white **snow geese** nest in colonies of thousands on the Arctic tundra. In winter they fly south, to areas like the Gulf of Mexico.

GUESS WHAT?...

The Arctic tern makes a round trip of about 20,000 miles each year—probably the longest migration of any bird.

Arctic terns lay their eggs in huge colonies on beaches and rocks during the Arctic summer. As winter approaches, the terns fly south all the way to the Antarctic in time for summer in the Southern Hemisphere.

Rearing young

Bellowing male **moose** lock antlers in fierce fights to win mates. The female gives birth to one calf, sometimes twins, which she feeds for about six months. The calf stays with its mother for about a year, until it has learned to fend for itself.

Life is always dangerous for young animals and birds, but nowhere is it more difficult than in the polar regions. Parents have to protect their babies against not only predators but also the extreme cold. The milk of some polar animals, like seals, is particularly fatty and rich so their young can grow quickly and get strong enough to survive the harsh conditions.

Some of the most devoted of all parents live at the Poles. Male emperor penguins don't eat for almost three months while they keep their eggs warm until they hatch.

Like all whales, the **white whale** gives birth to its young in the water. The mother takes very good care of her baby and feeds it for at least a year.

Southern giant petrels nest on the ground on Antarctic coasts and islands. If the nest is in danger, the petrel defends itself by spitting out bad-smelling oil from its beak. Even baby petrels can protect themselves this way.

Young petrels

92

The **tundra swan** lays her eggs in a nest of leaves and moss. The nest is lined with soft, downy feathers to help keep the eggs warm.

GUESS WHAT?...

❄ **The emperor penguin must keep its egg warm through the bitter Antarctic winter.**

The female emperor penguin lays her egg at the beginning of winter. Her mate then keeps the egg warm by rolling it onto his feet and covering it with a flap of skin on his belly. When the chick hatches, the male still keeps it safe and warm on his feet for a few weeks.

Baby **harp seals** grow fast feeding on their mother's rich milk. When only two weeks old, the baby weighs three times as much as it did at birth and has a thick layer of blubber to protect it from the cold. Soon after this, the mother harp seal leaves her baby to fend for itself and find its own food.

Index